LALANGUE, SINTHOME, JOUISSANCE, AND NOMINATION

LALANGUE, SINTHOME, JOUISSANCE, AND NOMINATION

A Reading Companion and Commentary on Lacan's *Seminar XXIII* on the *Sinthome*

Raul Moncayo

KARNAC

First published in 2017 by
Karnac Books Ltd
118 Finchley Road
London NW3 5HT

British Library Cataloguing in Publication Data

A C.I.P. for this book is available from the British Library

ISBN-13: 978-1-78220-424-4

Typeset by Medlar Publishing Solutions Pvt Ltd, India

Printed in Great Britain by TJ International Ltd, Padstow, Cornwall

www.karnacbooks.com

The Borromean knot of three that needs to be undone.

> If you find somewhere something, that schematizes the
> relationship of the Imaginary, Symbolic, and Real, qua
> separated from one another [...] with their relationship
> flattened out you already have the possibility of link-
> ing them by what? By the *sinthome*. (Lacan, session 1,
> *Seminar XXIII*)

See the following images.

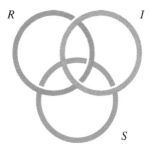

Figure 1. Untied knot.

Readers interested in Lacan's work are used to viewing the topological Borromean knot of three (below) knotted in such a way that if you untie one of the registers the other two become immediately untied.

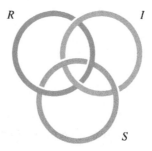

Figure 2. Knot of three.

In this seminar Lacan presents an untied knot that needs to be re-knotted by the *sinthome*. In the image above, the rings are laying one on top of the other. This idea pervades the entire seminar. Lacanians often interpret this version of the knot of four as being representative of psychosis and its reparation/suppletion via the *sinthome*. However, in the course of the seminar Lacan will also present a different knot of three and four rings as a specific example of psychosis. The knot of three for psychosis presents the Real tied to the Symbolic but on the flat plane the Imaginary lays untied on top of them.

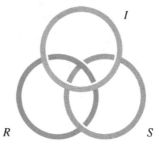

Figure 3. Knot of three psychosis.

In the knot of four for psychosis the *sinthome* ties the Imaginary to the other two while the Imaginary still remains loose and untied despite the *sinthome* holding it to a Borromean structure.

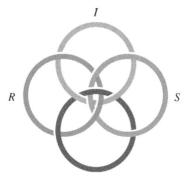

Figure 4. Knot of four psychosis.

In addition, Lacan says that in the case of psychosis, the supplementation and nomination provided by the *sinthome* (the fourth ring), coincides with the best results that can be expected from the practice of analysis. Since most analyses are of neurotics, this book advances the thesis that there are two knots of four (the first with untied rings, and the second with the untied Imaginary), one for neurosis and one for psychosis. The knot below is the knot of four for neurosis.

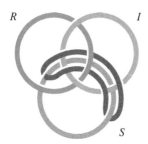

Figure 5. Knot of four neurosis.

This formulation should shed some light on the question raised by some whether Lacan, like Joyce, also had a psychotic structure for which his work was a *sinthome*. Otherwise, if the distinction between the two knots of four is collapsed this may lead to the paradoxical conclusion that only psychosis may reach the logical end of analysis.

CONTENTS

ABOUT THE AUTHOR

Raul Moncayo is supervising analyst, founding member, and faculty of the San Francisco Bay Area Lacanian School of Psychoanalysis (LSP). He has a private practice of psychoanalysis, psychotherapy, supervision, and consultation. He is visiting professor and adjunct faculty both in the US and other countries. Dr. Moncayo is former director of training for a large psychiatric clinic for the City of San Francisco, and the author of five books and multiple papers published in professional journals.

PREFACE

This reading companion and commentary on Lacan's *Seminar XXIII* is based on a series of talks that I gave over the course of a year at Hampshire College in Massachusetts in the years 2013 and 2014. The seminar was co-organised by the Lacanian School of Psychoanalysis and Annie Rogers, a professor of psychoanalytic studies at Hampshire College's School of Critical Social Enquiry. This book is meant to provide an analysis of Lacan's seminar but does not purport to provide an exhaustive line-by-line reading of a very complex and varied seminar. Rather it selects key themes of Lacanian theory that are found present throughout his work. In addition, I don't seek to simplify Lacan's ambiguous style, leaving the text open to different interpretations, while providing a theory that holds some lines of analysis into some of Lacan's important insights.

At first we read Lacan and we don't find what he calls the "easy way" into the seminar. We read the words but do not understand. But at some point this non-understanding produces what Lacan calls a Real cool heat lantern that turns not-understanding into understanding and "non-understanding". May this book light a lantern for the readers to guide their way through the text. The Real cool lantern is linked to how Joyce uses the term epiphany. Epiphany is a practice of writing or an experience that leaves language unknotted and without a meaning-generating context that leads to comprehension. Nevertheless, incomprehension in time may produce an epiphany or a lantern that opens an easy way into a "non-understanding" that is a form of understanding.

I also wish to acknowledge the contributions of Magdalena Romanowicz and Annie Rogers who co-taught this seminar with me and with whom I had many conversations on the topics under consideration. Magdalena was especially helpful with the topological figures she presented to our gracious participants. Together we developed the topological idea of there being two different forms of the knot of four specific to neurosis and psychosis. I also wish to thank the talented students at Hampshire College, members of the local psychoanalytic and College community and the members of the Lacanian School who participated online.

I also want to thank Cormac Gallagher for his permission to use his unedited translation of *Seminar XXIII* including many of its topological figures, and the late Roberto Harari whose introductory text ("How James Joyce made his Name") to *Seminar XXIII* proved to be an invaluable resource for this project.

Finally, this book is not about Joyce the writer, but more about the use that Lacan makes of Joyce, not to apply psychoanalysis to a literary subject, but rather to use the literary text to illustrate and develop psychoanalytic theory and Lacanian theory in particular. In no way does this work presume that Joyce's work can be limited to psychoanalytic or Lacanian ideas. It is an analysis of topology and language, or a *linguisterie* as Lacan called it, for clinicians. The references to neurosis and psychosis are always there. However, a Lacanian clinic can also be of use to those interested in literary theory and/or social studies to develop theory within their own respective fields of studies.

With respect to the Lacanian clinic, there is no direct correspondence between clinical facts or symptoms, analytic practice, and the truths presented at the level of the theory. Analytic practice is what bridges the apparent independence of the theory and clinical facts and symptoms. Many of the cases and clinical material presented will be those drawn from literary sources, Freud's cases well known to psychoanalysis and the public, and clinical vignettes derived from my own practice.

Nowadays it is more difficult to present detailed case studies because this requires informed consent from analysands and not simply protecting their identity as used to be the case. Analysts also consider counterproductive to reveal to analysands the details of their analysis. Behaviourists object to this by saying that evidence shows that informed consent has no discernible impact on the treatment and even if it does the impact may be positive or not that significant. However, the material worked on in analysis is significantly different from the symptoms and narrative discussed in behavioural psychotherapy. Analytic material, for example, involves themes related to sexual and aggressive fantasies that may raise many more concerns regarding confidentiality and public reputations. This is specially the case for analysands who are also in the process of professional and analytical formation.

Lacanian theory and analysis does not focus so much on conscious narratives and the grammatical aspects of speech. The latter has more to do with the normative Code and syntaxes that regulate the signifying chains or connections between words, or between the signifier and the signified. Lacanian analysis privileges the upper vector in the graph of desire (see Romanowicz & Moncayo, 2015) that represents an unconscious signifying chain in the Freudian sense, as well as in the Lacanian sense of the non-sense or senselessness of the Real unconscious as manifest within the language of the unconscious or *lalangue*. This Real unconscious is also revealed in mathematical and topological structures that underlie and support the structures and appearance of psychical phenomena.

The unconscious requires a different dimension of reason (Nous) and non-knowing, that nonetheless is still linked with the other three Aristotelian categories: Episteme, Techne, and practical Reason. Lacanian discourse uses the four Aristotelian forms of reason in particular and implicit ways: Nous; the Real as practical reason, praxis or the psychoanalytic act; Episteme that includes both formal and critical Reason, contradiction and non-contradiction; and Techne that includes the psychoanalytic method of the talking cure and free association. To Freud's method, Lacan adds the scansion of speech and of the session.

Nous represents the relationship between knowing and doubt, or knowing and non-knowing as sources of knowledge (I only know that I don't know). In addition, Nous represents the contemplation of the first principles. Episteme is how we think about valid knowledge and the relationships between theory and practice or theory and method, etc. Techne is method or experiment, and technology (that includes the use of the phone and the internet within psychoanalysis).

Anglo-American empiricism within the social sciences uses random sampling, control groups, questionnaires, formal logic, and the statistics of approximation, but only works with Episteme as formal reason, and Techne. Non-statistical social science works with Episteme as dialectical and critical reason, Nous, and practical reason. Both of these forms of knowledge stem from the Western intellectual tradition but in the final analysis empiricism rejects the other forms of reason as invalid or not based on random sampling, and evidence-based forms of knowledge. The same is not true the other way around. Anglo-American science and cognitive science tends to reject continental European thought or relegates it to the humanities. Since England is part of Europe, and provided a safe harbour for Freud and psychoanalysis, it tends to take a less extreme position against psychoanalysis as that found in the United States in this day and age. Several universities in England have departments of psychoanalysis, while none exist in the United States.

The question of which type of reason is rejecting another form of reason in actuality translates into the question of the relationship among power, economics (resources), and knowledge. But of course it is critical reason that is capable of making this observation. Otherwise the conflict could be easily resolved by giving each form of reason a place in academic discourse. Empiricists are often surprised as to why psychoanalysts and other intellectuals criticise the exclusive use of empiricism within the social sciences as if this meant in some way a general rejection of scientific thought or method especially in the natural sciences. Empiricism seems to be unable to acknowledge how empiricism has established itself as a dominant discourse within the social sciences to the exclusion of other forms of reason.

It is also interesting that although the four types of reason come from Aristotle, the sharp separation between the pre-Socratic dialectical logic of contradiction and the formal logic of non-contradiction also comes from Aristotle. However, in the last centuries German thought signalled a return to the pre-Socratics as seen in the philosophical works of Hegel, Nietzsche, Heidegger, Gadamer, and more importantly in the theorists associated with the Frankfurt school. I say more importantly, because German thought, as reflected in the Frankfurt school of critical theory, continued a German tradition without the taint of German nationalism associated with Nazism (as seen in Heidegger's early career, for example). The Frankfurt school, and Hegel in particular, also inspired an entire generation of French thinkers associated with structuralism, post-structuralism, deconstructionism, and post-modernism that represented an intellectual climate and context surrounding and contributing to the development of Lacan's thought.

The principle of non-contradiction says that you cannot both be and not be at the same time. One of the two statements has to be either true or false. You are either alive or dead and this is quite consistent with ordinary common sense. On the other hand, there are some people who say they feel dead while alive and when people die they continue to live in the minds/ hearts of their loved ones or through their legacies. Scholars will usually respond to this objection by saying that the particular cases where the principle of non-contradiction may not hold are metaphorical or allegorical/symbolic examples of the order of sense or metaphor rather than objective reference. This distinction in turn is consistent with the hermeneutic tradition that argues that there is a different logic for the natural sciences and the human sciences (objectivity versus interpretation). However, most scientists do not accept this distinction thus showing a split within science, European culture, and knowledge itself. The political/economic struggles over hegemony and power in relationship to knowledge take place within this split. In addition, new developments in contemporary multi-valued logic (that includes formal and dialectical logic) such as paraconsistent logic and *dialetheism* argue that there can be particular true contradictions without invalidating the principle of non-contradiction.

The question of metaphor and sense in language, that is so relevant for the humanities, literature, even narratives and statements within science, reveals a split between metaphor and mathematics, concepts and numbers. Mathematicians often object to metaphoric transposition from mathematics to non-mathematical or non-arithmetical premises or axioms. Such transposition can be considered a residue of the Pythagoric yearnings of antiquity to use mathematics to speculate about non-mathematical theory. This argument is used to protect the validity and specificity of science and formal logic and the principle of non-contradiction as the right pathway to true and socially acceptable valid knowledge. What lies outside science is relegated to philosophy and the relevance of philosophy is very much in question in contemporary society. Even within philosophy, Anglo-American analytical philosophy wants to restrict philosophy to the philosophy of science or the philosophy that supports scientific or pragmatic endeavour.

However, the argument has not been settled by any means, since many questions still remain as to the relationship between mathematics and logic, among language, mathematics, and logic, and the differences among concepts, metaphors, numbers, objects, and things. Numbers are not metaphors yet metaphors may reach the Real, experience, and jouissance in ways that numbers may not. The metaphor of emptiness and the null set represents what is not identical to number or is beyond the concept of number and neither exists nor does not exist. Mathematics needs logic yet the premises or axioms of logic are not the same as mathematics or are not always arithmetical in nature. Conversely, the axioms of mathematics are not always logical or arithmetical either. For example, the square root of -1 known as an imaginary number contradicts arithmetical principles (every negative number multiplied by itself yields a positive number) and yet is widely used within arithmetical systems ($2i + 3i = 5i$). The same applies to set theory as a way to understand natural numbers that many natural scientists reject in favour of the common sense description of natural numbers as 1,2,3,4, etc.

Another key example of the difference between mathematics and logic is the logical premise that $0 = 1$ because zero is the first number or unit and this premise conflicts with the arithmetical axiom that $0 \neq 1$, or in set-theoretic terms $0 = \emptyset$ and $1 = \{\emptyset\}$. But, because of the null set concept within set theory, zero does not only represent the absence of an object or a concept but a number (the empty set) that is present in all numbers. Thus zero is equivalent (but not identical) to the one unit because zero as the first number is present in all numbers or sets ($\emptyset \in x$). The reverse is not true because any number cannot be in zero since zero denotes the absence of numbers. In set theory beginning with the empty set you can use the same number or no-number ($\emptyset$) to describe the unity of natural numbers or their ordering by succession. By the same token parentheses are used to increase the number or set $\varnothing + 1 = \{\varnothing\}$. Zero or the empty set is a 1 number or unit that is present in all numbers and their order of succession and at the same time $\varnothing + 1$ can be used to derive all numbers and the differences between them. There is a 1 that contains 0 and a 1 that does not. In computer science there is the binary bit that is either 1 or 0 and the quantum Q'bit 1 that contains or is a superposition of 1 and 0.

Finally, the null set is not a concept, or it is a number that is not a number, and therefore is not identical to itself, yet through the empty set or the concept of zero, the null set becomes a number. The null set as a non-number retains the quality and pathos of emptiness, jouissance, affect, or thought, that says more than zero or numbers, or words for that matter. For Heidegger, following Kierkegaard, nothingness defined as absence is revealed as anxiety or anguish. In a second moment anxiety founds the logical no, rather than the other way around. This is one of the reasons that Lacan said that anxiety is the only Real affect that does not lie. However, emptiness can also be revealed as a still and serene presence that constitutes the opposite of anxiety and which is often used to treat anxiety (in behavioural treatments).

At some point both human experience and mathematics need metaphors and symbols/letters (i.e., Phi or Φ, arithmetically known as 1.618...) to put a stop to the bad infinity of irrational numbers or to the impossible quest to represent experience through numbers. On the other hand, numbers, and non-standard numbers in particular (infinitesimals and imaginary numbers, for example), can reach truth and the Real beyond the capability or the reach of language, metaphors, knowledge, and the Symbolic. The ratio for the golden number (Phi and phi) can be found in music and in the form and structure of nature. Both numbers and metaphors have the ability to go beyond one another.

Can the same thing be said about formal symbolic systems? Can the structure of the signifier and metaphor, for example, be decided on the basis of an arithmetical ratio between metaphors or between metaphors and the experiences within the Real of experience that they represent? Is the function of measure present within the signifier as a unit? Does repetition and substitution occur as a function of countable units (real numbers) equidistant from one another and on the basis of which mathematical operations could take place? Is human irrationality beyond numbers or exactly represents a family of numbers needed to comprehend the irrational in the human psyche?

In the first unary numeral system there were unary strokes or writing but no code, order, or concept of number as seen in natural numbers and prime numbers. In *Seminar XIV* Lacan says that the function of the signifier has a golden proportion that envelops or overlaps with the *objet a* or phi. With irrational numbers, the regression, repetition, and distribution of signifiers and trivial zeros representing the lack (and its reparation) is infinite. This argument seems to give support to the premise that the unconscious and its objects/signifiers are not without number or beyond number. The capital Phi function of metaphor and castration converts the irrational into something rational (Phi $(1.681...)$–phi $(0.681...) = 1$) and the lack into a Real void. Can the Real void and the null set be reached through a different family of numbers or only through something inconceivable within jouissance and experience?

In a previous book (Moncayo & Romanowicz, 2015) we tried to combine both approaches through the use of imaginary numbers (in the mathematical sense) and the zeta function that yields non-trivial zeros and prime numbers. True holes and prime numbers can be linked to the Real unconscious and the distribution of new signifiers, and the emergence of new names and metaphors. There may be a singular code for each Real singular subject. Gödel transposed letters in a text into figures and values. But the assignment of number to a text or a signifier was arbitrary. What the assignation does is to turn a symbolic statement into an arithmetical statement that is true within mathematics but the correspondence between symbols and numbers and between symbols/numbers and experience/ jouissance is contingent, if not arbitrary. Something Real about what metaphors represent may be equally lost in mathematical transposition or metaphoric representation.

Thus, we cannot transpose a proof in a formal arithmetical system into a proof in a formal symbolic system (or vice versa), because something of the object, thing, or being may be lost in the process. If we transpose numbers into metaphors, then something Real about numbers may be lost; on the other hand, if we transpose metaphors into numbers, something Real about metaphor may be equally lost. Thus, at some point we may only justify our axioms, and thereby our proofs, by infor- mal means, whatever these may be (including mathematical thought). Proofs and arguments may be intuitively clear and convincing, or they may be useful in practice, or they may be consistent with established tradition. Any of these criterions may be used by way of justification.

Finally, practical reason refers to ethics, how we think about ethics (of desire or morality), to professional practices, but more fundamentally to the psychoanalytic act that brings the dimension of the cut and of the Real into a session. For the Greeks the first principles emanate from Nous and it is this type of reason or faculty of mind that theoretical discussions strengthen and inspire at the time of their occurrence. Nous is a term for the faculty of the human mind that is necessary for understanding what is true or Real.

The phenomena that we study contribute to the awareness (Nous) which remains independent and undefined by the con- tent of what is learned or who is doing the learning. Aristotle (*De Anima, Book III*, Hicks, 1907) referred to it as separate, and as being without attributes and unmixed. As such it constitutes a link between the known, the unknown, and the unknowable.

In many ways it corresponds to what Freud called the free-floating awareness of the analyst without a specific subject or object. This definition of Nous avoids the paradox of referring to an unconscious awareness although Lacan does speak of unknown knowing or *"l'insu qui sait"*. When an analyst is in the presence of his or her patient's speech the quality of *Nous* will also be there with the analyst. And although the analyst may not be thinking of the theory, the first principles that matter will also be there for his or her disposition and use.

Introduction

The relationship between Lacan's Seminar III *on psychosis and his* Seminar XXIII *on the* sinthome

The unconscious, foreclosure, the question of Being, the signifier in the Real, are all terms that in one way or another are present in both seminars although they are twenty years apart.

In *Seminar III* (1955–1956), according to Lacan, the psychotic subject does have an unconscious. This contrasts sharply with the usual psychoanalytic notion that for the psychotic subject there is no repression and the unconscious is all manifest or predominates. In this formulation, repression and the reality ego that make the secondary process and cohesive speech possible, are both missing in psychosis. In the neurotic the unconscious is created through repression, but in psychosis repression fails. But for Lacan although there is no primary repression, in psychosis there is still another defence at play. In psychosis the unconscious is created through foreclosure.

The concept of foreclosure follows from Freud's notion that psychotics repudiate reality and try to replace it. In the case of Schreber, Freud (1911c) used different terms for the defence involved in psychoses, including *Verwerfung* or foreclosure. The primary and secondary process, the unconscious, the preconscious, and consciousness are all structured or disarticulated by the intervention of a defence, whether primary repression or foreclosure.

1

According to Lacan what prevents primary repression from being established is the foreclosure (thrown out of the symbolic order) of the Name of the Father (NoF). In the defence known as foreclosure, the NoF, as the source of primary repression, is not simply repressed. In neurosis the repressed/repressive unconscious structures the perception of the internal and external worlds through metaphor and metonymy, as well as the relationship between images and words. In psychosis the foreclosed NoF is found within what Lacan calls the Real unconscious. The Real unconscious itself includes two aspects: 1. The Real unconscious refers to the never signified imperceptible unknown or unknowable internal and external worlds; and 2. The Real unconscious contains the foreclosed signifier/signified of the NoF that returns from the unmarked dimension of the external world (for example, the sound of ocean waves commanding and speaking to the psychotic subject).

Repressed unconscious	Real unconscious	
Repressed/repressive unconscious that structures the perception of the internal and external worlds through metaphor and metonymy, words and images	The never signified imperceptible unknown or unknowable internal and external worlds	The foreclosed internal signified that returns through the unmarked dimension of the perception of the external world

The foreclosure of the NoF leaves a hole or scotoma in the field of psychotic perception. In *Seminar XXIII* this hole has to be repaired through the supplementation and nomination associated with the *sinthome*.

The unconscious in psychosis involves a failure in the program/knot that articulates the relationship between language and perception. According to Freud (1894a) the unconscious in psychosis is found in perception rather than thinking or wishing, or acting out (as in neurosis and perversion).

The NoF is what inoculates the neurotic subject against paranoia and psychosis. For example, a father could say to his son: "Never take your two eyes from the world. I didn't make the world that I left you in." The son is to bow to roses the father cultivated within a world he did not make. The gaze of the father mediates the way the son looks at the world and makes it a safer and less persecuting place. He also tells him that he did not make the world he left him in. This second statement undoes the omnipotence of the father by placing the father in relationship to a symbolic world that pre-existed the father. The son bows to the world via the mediation of the father.

In psychosis the NoF returns from the Real in the form of the subject feeling chosen for a persecution that is also a sign of distinction. The persecution is an imaginary form of the negative originally involved with the NoF that was foreclosed. But because of foreclosure, in psychoses there is no metaphor only a concrete substitution. The benevolence of the NoF is not there to provide protection against persecution; instead the subject is exposed to the raw and profane phallic attribute of the Other and to the mother's desire. In the clinic we can see this in patients who feel chosen and persecuted by a powerful brutal Other who wants to hurt them or wants to use them as an object for their enjoyment.

To explain psychosis Lacan proposes the premise that behind the process of verbalisation there is a primordial *Bejahung*, an admission of the Symbolic, which itself can be missing in psychoses. Lacan here is following Freud who saw psychopathology as a way to learn something about the structure of the psyche and not only about specific forms of psychopathology.

This method is part and parcel of Lacan's interest in the study of psychoses.

> It can happen that a subject refuses access to his symbolic world to something that he has nevertheless experienced, which in this case is nothing other than the threat of castration. (Lacan, 1955–1956, p. 12)
>
> [...] there is a stage at which it is possible for a portion of symbolization not to take place. It can thus happen that something primordial regarding the subject's being (note the reference to being here) does not enter into symbolization and is not repressed, but rejected. (Lacan, 1955–1956, p. 81)

The affirmation at the base of symbolisation refers to the NoF as a primordial signifier. Presumably this is something that has not happened for the psychotic either structurally or developmentally but does routinely take place for the "normal" neurotic as a necessary developmental step in the construction of psychical/mental subjective structure. The affirmation of the NoF refers to the symbolization/representation of the presence of the father, to the presence of the father in the mother's mind, but more importantly perhaps to the symbolization of the absence of the mother (bad breast) and the function that both of these play in the development of language and the symbolic order.

In *The Ego and the Id* Freud (1923b) claims that identification with the father of individual pre-history is prior to and more primary than the relationship to the object. The paternal metaphor prior to an object relation with the mother refers to Freud's notion of a primal identification with the father of individual pre-history. However, in Freud this idea is linked to identification in the mode of a primitive form of oral incorporation or eating of the primal father as a mythical philogenetic inheritance carried over from the primal horde that killed and ate the father. When making contact with the breast and the incorporation of milk, and given that the breast in the mother's mind as an *objet a* could also function as a substitute for the paternal phallus, the child is not only incorporating the breast but also the primal father or the mother's own father for that matter. This would be one way of understanding the identification with the father of individual pre-history. However, Freud also says that this happens prior to any object relation and as we see in this example the identification with the father takes place in relationship to the breast even prior to a subject–object distinction.

So Lacan's thesis of an affirmation of the NoF as a primordial signifier at the base of symbolisation seems to be a better way to understand the identification with the father of personal pre-history. The father of the child is already symbolised or not in the mother's mind. In addition, the child perceives a third presence whether in the actual figure of the father or in the mother's own mind. The NoF is a metaphor for the presence of the father in the child's life and mind, of the symbol of the father in the mother's mind, as well as what helps symbolise the absence of the breast, as a placeholder for the loss of the fantasy object that the mother is for the child (breast-*objet a*) and that the child is for the mother (imaginary phallus).

The affirmation of the NoF is bound up with the absence of the mother and the acceptance of the negative as a necessary moment. Thus, Lacan links the affirmation of the NoF with the acceptance of symbolic castration. Conversely, the affirmation of the NoF and the absence of the mother can both be negated. The love for the father and the function of the father has to be understood within this context more than the father simply representing another mother, attachment object, or caregiver.

In this way both the NoF and the absence of the mother become representatives of negation and the phallic function of castration. It is not that the subject has been threatened with castration, but that castration is the name for the imaginary mass of feelings, sounds, and ideas that the subject may experience in relationship to the presence of the NoF and the absence of the object. The NoF symbolically castrates/negates the subject as an imaginary phallus of the mother and castrates the mother's imaginary phallus (that the child represents).

The NoF as a primordial affirmation is also at the same time a form of negation. Thus admission is a better term to represent the acceptance of the NoF as a term that is also an affirmation of the desire of the mother and its object, and at the same time an admission of *symbolic* castration or the loss of the mother and the object. The NoF is a positive mark of the negative and this is what qualifies the NoF as a unary trace on which the symbolic system is built. The NoF is a positive term and at the same time a unary form of negation that leaves the negated object unmarked. The unary trace is a term that Lacan borrowed from mathematics following Freud's use of the unary trait to explain a form of identification.

> The unary numeral system is the simplest numeral system to represent natural numbers. In order to represent the concept of number, an arbitrary notch, stroke, trait, trace, vertical bar, or a tally mark written "|" or "/" is repeated N times. For example, using the tally mark "|", the number 4 is represented as "||||". (Moncayo & Romanowicz, 2015, p. 105)

Once established, the unary trace becomes a system of non-diacritical marks that are not yet integers. In the history of the species, the unary trace arose as a positive mark for an absence or the killing of an animal or the menstruation of a woman that indicated she was not pregnant. Both events are linked to survival, reproduction, and loss. The absence of life gives life and the possibility of enumerating and counting the forms of life. Life forms and the birth and death of animals and humans could now be counted. Prior to counting births or deaths with unary marks or traces there were no marks or objects and therefore a form of Real outside representation. With the unary trace the Real goes into birth and death and begins to be counted and oriented within a system of marks.

The NoF as a unary trace will orient the nascent subject in the field of signification. The subject is marked with the unary trace of the signifier in the field of the Other. The unary trace has the ability to orient itself on the infinite straight line in relation to other traits that later (with the advent of zero) will become numbers and signifiers. The unary trace is what all signifiers have in common. Zero first appears as the act of making a trace that indicates the absence of a mark but also the absence of marks before the mark was instated (the empty set and the null set respectively). Zero at this point is not yet a discrete concept.

The unary trace is both a unary negation of the Real or of the absence of representation or the unmarked and at the same time presents something of the Real. The Real before the mark was the mythical and philogenetic original state of affairs when the world was experienced without concepts or marks. A unary form of negation has the characteristic of appearing as an affirmative mark while at the same time what is negated is unmarked or without an object (the unary mark that negates the unmarked that has now been marked).

In the case of the NoF as a unary trace the Real stands for the outside representation, the desire of the mother, and the object of the mother's desire. The NoF negates the Real or the no-mark and generates the boundary out of which the Real can be presented as well as signifies the desire of the mother that will from then on be represented as a metonymical signified for what the NoF negates. What the NoF negates/represents is the Real and the object of the mother's desire, two different forms of the Real therefore (that coincide with the two defini- tions of the Real in the early and late Lacan).

The NoF as a unary trace will first come to represent an anterior loss of infinite or immortal Life prior to conception and later will come to represent the loss of the union with the mother and the object that represents such union.

> The relation to the Other is precisely that which, for us, brings out what is represented by the lamella [...] the relation between the living subject and that which he loses by having to pass, for his reproduction, through the sexual cycle. (Lacan, *Seminar XI*, 1964, p. 199)
>
> It is the libido, qua pure life instinct, that is to say immortal life [...]. It is precisely what is subtracted from the living being by virtue of the fact that it is subject to the cycle of sexual reproduction. And it is of this that all the forms of the *objet a* that can be enumerated are the representatives, the equivalents. The placenta [...] may serve to symbolize the most profound lost object. (Ibid., p. 198)

Immortal life and its loss is represented by the lack in the Other or the NoF in the field of the signifier, and in the body the loss is represented by the placenta which then itself is lost. At the same time this loss will generate the wish for the breast as an *objet a*, for the part object of the mother, and for the desire of the mother.

It is important to distinguish among hunger, tenderness, reproduction, and sexual desire, because the need for the breast, for example, is also a form of hunger that Freud initially understood as a self-preservation and life-preservation drive. In addition, Freud (1912d) also spoke of early maternal tenderness that for him constituted a separate manifestation of a non-sexual drive. Winnicott (1963/2011, p. 176) in the object relation school focused on the adequate environment and the good-enough mother by which he means the maternal preoccupation and care-taking behaviour of the environmental mother. Then he speaks of the object mother by which he means how the child functions as a fantasy object for the mother as well as vice versa.

Freud instead starts out with maternal tenderness and Lacan with the question of the desire of the mother. Rene Spitz (1945) with his studies on hospitalism showed that adequate care-taking behaviour is necessary but not sufficient for an infant. What Winnicott appears not to articulate is the desire of the mother although he does mention later on that the environment mother has a function of providing empathy to her child but this is described as an almost objective environmental quality. Wishing and desire appear only in relation to the object mother.

In mammals and evolution, maternal tenderness and the proximity and union or bond between mother and child is associated with the evolution of milk as a nutrient and a protective fluid derived from proteins. Milk feeding strengthened the mother–child bond as a foundation for maternal love. In addition, the development of the placenta as an organ inside the mother's body helped protect the fetus from predators. A new gene had to be acquired to make a new organ that would establish a new form of organic union between mother and child. The new gene evolved from a virus that had the capacity to suppress the immune system. What could cause an illness would also allow for the evolution of a new organ given that the immune system would have treated the fetus as an invader. Viruses attacking reproductive cells became part of a gene inside the cell nucleus out of which the placenta developed. This was an unpredictable leap in evolution. A virus that could lead to illness and death was transformed and mutated into a gene and organ with life preservation properties. But is such mutation really unpredictable and random or follows a constructive logic and determinism associated with an enigmatic Life drive?

In his drive theory, Freud used the concept of "anaclisis" to account for how the sexual drive in humans is derived from a biological self-preservation instinct. The drive acquires a significant independence once it becomes established within a symbolic/psychical order. The notion of a psychical drive as distinct from a biological instinct develops out of the prototype of the experience of satisfaction whereby in the process of satisfying biological needs for nutrition and growth, a jouissance develops in the infant linked to the satisfaction itself, independent from the needs of the biological organism. Now this satisfaction remains inextricably linked to the other as *objet a*. The *objet a* as an object of the imagination and fantasy is transformed into a virus that haunts the psychical system in the form of thinking that itself will have to be transformed into higher order thinking with the acquisition of language and the paternal function. This holds true for both the mother and the infant. The mother can also use the infant as an object to satisfy her own narcissism independently from what may be nourishing or healthy for a child.

What could be called a self-preservation ego drive leading to the acquisition of independent hunting skills in animals (instrumental reason), initially supported and made possible by maternal care becomes a basis for the operation of a killing machine that seems to be the opposite of maternal care and protection. Animals will kill not only when hungry or for immediate survival purposes but as a way to protect the control of their territory and its objects. Human beings will also do the same but in addition they will seek pleasure and objects independently from life preservation needs. This is the virus that gets re-introduced into life preserving processes.

In human beings and symbolic systems, it is the NoF and the paternal function that functions as a brake and an inhibition that mutates the "virus" that operates within the Imaginary register, object love, and the sexual drive. This formulation, of course, does not deny the fact that language may require a particular form of gene (FOXP2) and DNA letter (T) that will affect the structure of the neural brain network but not the structure of language itself. In turn, desire, as a motivation for action in the world, will function within the parameters set by a symbolic system. It is the NoF that, in relationship to the desire of the mother and maternal care and preoccupation, will suppress the "virus" at work within the object of the mother and child's desire. Such virus, in the form of the imaginary *objet a* and phallus, is a metaphor for what remains repressed under primary repression.

With his second theory of drives, Freud (1920g) reinforced a connection between tenderness as a primary form of object relation and the ego drives or narcissism. He calls both of them libido (object libido and ego libido) although libido for Freud was not just psychic energy but was sexual in nature. In his first theory of drives he included a non-sexual drive as an ego drive he associated with tenderness and that later on in life (after adolescence) was supposed to fuse with the sexual drive and the genital relation. The two drives are fused when adults leave their parents' home and cling to their spouses instead, with whom they also have a sexual life.

Within Freud's second theory of drives and with the notion of object libido it is unclear what happens to the early form of tenderness as a non-sexual form of parental love. It is also unclear how a primary form of object libido prior to any form of ego could also be an ego drive. It seems that the connecting or linking function of the Life drive would be more primal than a self-preservation ego drive. Either life is a larger category that includes the sexual drive and the ego drive or every form of the life drive and ego drive is a derivative of the sexual drive. In humans the latter could not be the case given that the sexual drive, as distinct from biological reproduction, could lead to premature death, illness, and destruction. In his final theory of drives Freud argued the former since Eros included the life-preservation drives and the sexual drive. Now what unifies the subject is Eros or the life drive rather than the ego drives and the ego or sexual drives can work for the Life or Death drive.

This problem is also reflected in the theory of sublimation where sublimation is both an aim-inhibited drive and a direct satisfaction or manifestation of Eros. In adult love such as that found between the future parents of a child, the sexual drive and the feelings of tenderness are fused, although originally they could function separately. With a new-born or new life, the two forms are again found separate only to be re-joined later on, and so on and so forth.

These considerations point to the fact that the desire of the mother and its object has more than one signification. The child is an object of tenderness, as well as a part object cause of the mother's desire. What is this object of tenderness? Where does the tenderness of the mother and of the child come from if not from the narcissism of the mother that is the same thing as saying that the child is a fantasy object or an imaginary phallus for the mother?

Narcissism and the sexual drive cannot be separated as Freud (1914c) discovered in his studies on narcissism that led to the reformulation of drive theory. It is difficult to escape the conclusion that there are two types of fusion or two types of One, a fusion or indifferentiation in the Real and a fusion in the Imaginary that are homogenous and yet different from one another. The fusion in the Imaginary includes the fusion between mother and child through the fantasy object, and the apprehension of the body image as a total form of narcissism and the ideal ego. In imaginary oneness, the Real is supplanted or co-opted by the Imaginary. The empty mirror is replaced or represented by the images it reflects. Here we have 0 as 1 or the first number, and 0 as different from 1 or even from the concept of zero because zero is the number non-identical with itself. The presence of the Real as the absence of signifying elements, is replaced by the totality of the image, and appears within the Symbolic as both the signifier of a lack or the lack of a signifier and as a synchronic place of articulation and disarticulation for the structure. The signifier contains zero and the image does not while the Real is a plenum or a presence beyond signification.

The distinction between the two forms of the One parallels the separation between tender union between mother and child and the child and mother fusion through the object of fantasy. The Real outside representation continues in the desire of the mother in the form of the enigmatic feeling of tenderness under consideration (associated with the enigma of life itself), and in the field of signification the desire of the mother has the imaginary phallus as the signified for the signifier of the NoF. In utero both forms of the One are fused but with birth the life drive splits into the enigmatic affect of tenderness and the object libido associated with the sexual drive.

Eventually the two forms of the One or the Life drive, according to Freud's developmental perspective, will be fused again under so-called normal genital conditions. But as the phenomenon of "normal" or ordinary neurosis shows, relationships will remain vulnerable to the split between tenderness without sex or sex without tenderness. This is one reason why Lacan says that there is no sexual relation and Freud (1912d) says that speaking beings are prone to desire those they don't love or don't depend on and love or depend on those they don't desire. This state of affairs explains many unhappy marriages or unions and infidelities within married or coupled life. In passing, it should be noted that ironically in order to avoid the peril of normal neurosis (or character neurosis), Freud (1912d) recommends a normalisation of perverse fantasy (not perverse actions). To function sexually, it may be necessary to lose the horror of incest with a parent or sibling.

Would it be accurate to call the object of tenderness an *objet a*, since Lacan has also said that the *objet a* is *a*-sexual? The *objet a* is also the representative of an anterior loss that begins with the loss of infinite or immortal life through reproduction within a cycle conditioned by birth and death. Something of infinite life passes unto conditioned life in the form of the fusion of mother and child first in the body and then in the mind.

In utero the infant will be an a-sexual form of object or non-object that is not yet a subject. The umbilical cord and the placenta are the first forms of partial a-sexual objects that will be lost and will remain as emblements of the loss of infinite life. Although now physically separated, the psychical reunion between mother and child will take place according to different manifestations of the *objet a*. The *objet a* is an a-sexual object of tenderness and at the same time takes the form of the imaginary phallus, the imaginary and real aspects of the *objet a*, S_0 and S_1 respectively or two forms of S_1, one paired with S_0 (a-sexual) and the other pared with S_2 (NoF-imaginary phallus).

In the same way, the desire of the mother as a form of the Real outside the NoF differs from the desire of the mother as the signified of the NoF that has the imaginary phallus for its object. Both forms of the desire of the mother parallel the two senses of the NoF as a unary trace derived from the Real, and the NoF as the source of primary repression. The desire of the mother as a form of tenderness is linked to the NoF as a unary trace and the *objet a* in the Real while the NoF as the source of primary repression is linked to the signified of the imaginary phallus as the object cause of the mother's desire and the *objet a* in the Imaginary. The NoF associated with primary repression and negation, as well as the imaginary phallus and imaginary *objet a*, are manifestations of the separation effects and malevolent manifestations of the death drive and the jouissance of the Other. The death drive in its symbolic and imaginary forms (defences and wishes/fears) is both inevitable and necessary, and problematic at the same time.

The desire of the mother as the signified of the NoF will negate the negation emerging from the NoF by representing the Real outside signification and by representing objects of desire. The Real will remain unrepresented within desire, but now the NoF or the sign will be replaced by the presence of an object of desire, a movement that reverses the way that the first trace arose to represent the absence of an object (the sign replaces/ negates an object and the object replaces/negates the sign).

Conversely, the unary trace of the NoF will continue to appear in the loss/privation of the object/breast that the child has identified in relationship to the desire of the mother. Now the problem of frustration/privation/symbolic castration in relationship to the loss of the breast will appear in full force as Melanie Klein has described in her theory. According to Lacanian theory the ambivalence (love/hate) towards the breast as *objet a* will be stabilised with weaning and the appearance of the specular image beginning around six months of age.

The naming of the specular image in the mirror or the development of the ideal ego as a unified bodily image will come to compensate for the loss of the partial mother/breast by representing the total image of the body as the object cause of the mother's desire. Now the child will have its own image derived from the maternal object. However, there will also be a loss represented in this image, as a blank spot or hole or something missing associated with this image. This missing part in the image will represent the fact that the child may not be the only object of the mother's desire and that her desire is turned elsewhere. The acquisition of a body image will remain linked throughout life to the sense of something missing within the body image that serves as a basis for a faculty of self-criticism that has the body as its object.

The loss associated with the NoF and its signified in the form of the fantasised imaginary phallus object of the mother's desire will be compensated by the child's identification with its image in front of the mirror. Naming represents a gift but also will become the signifier of a loss at the level of the ideal ego. The loss and its symbolisation at the level of the ideal ego will then lead to the formation of the ego ideal when the Other appears as the object of the mother's desire.

But the compensatory act of naming, that gives the child a bodily identity, weakens the link between earlier losses

(the breast) and the earlier forms of the NoF as a unary negation in the pre-history of the subject. Once the unary negation
has been established, it is wind back or nullified as if it had
never happened. The NoF as a unary mark of the unmarked
becomes unmarked once again so to speak. Under primary
repression both the repressed and the repressive disappear and
can only be inferred from their effects, or deduced from basic
and intuitive axioms or explanatory principles. Such intuitive
principles may be counter-intuitive or at least not identical to
common sense.

The negation of the unary negation associated with the NoF
does not only produce a new signifier of desire but also sends
the NoF as a unary trace back to the Real within desire and
the signified outside representation. But to avoid psychosis the
NoF has to be used to access a unified image (the Other pointing to the image and saying you are so and so). A relationship
to the Name has to be established in order to retain a Real
immeasurable dimension beyond image and word that functions within the Borromean knot.

The signified for the first affirmative signifier of negation
(NoF) is the pure desire of the mother with its accompanying enigmatic sounds and feelings, as well as the object of the
mother's desire or the small phi (the imaginary *objet a*), which
in many instances might very well be the imaginary phallus.
These are the drives that will energise the libidinal representation of the body and the ideal ego. The NoF as a unary trace
of negation remains invisibly behind these developments,
unmarked as it were.

For Lacan, psychosis, as a disorder of language, consists of a
hole, or a lack at the level of the signifier produced by the foreclosure of the NoF. Such a hole is a tear in the net rather than
the holes that are always part of any net. As mentioned earlier,
the NoF as a unary trace orients the nascent subject in the field
of signification. The unary trace is what all signifiers have in
common. The unary trace has the ability to orient itself on the

infinite straight line in relation to other traits in the field of the Other. Here the NoF in relationship to the field of language and the battery of signifiers has a similar function as the null set that according to Frege (1903) constitutes a foundational stone for the construction of natural numbers (for more about this point please see Moncayo & Romanowicz, 2015).

> Null set used to be a common synonym for "empty set". Although there is still a lot of controversy around conceptualization of the two terms a very simple and satisfactory way of thinking about it for our purposes is that the empty set contains the null set and so although the empty set has no members in it a set is still a thing that has the "no-thing" in it. (p. 126)

Another way to think of the distinction between the null set (that for many mathematicians are the same thing) and the empty set is along the lines of the unary trace or the mark of the unmarked. The empty set is equivalent to the concept of zero as the first whole number. The unary numeral system did not have a concept of zero or of numbers. This could be symbolised by the symbol for the null set ($\emptyset$) that has a unary stroke negating the zero symbol. The unary trace is not yet a concept, because concepts require differentiation and the unary trace contains presence and absence at the same time. The null set is a concept beyond a concept, or a mark of the unmarked. There is no data available or no signified for what the null set or the unary trace represents.

The conceptual definition of the null set is represented by the empty set. There is a signified and data about the empty set because it indicates the absence of something specific (an object or a concept) or a set that has no members. The null set is the empty set that does not contain itself because otherwise it would not be empty. In this sense the empty set is not really empty. On the other hand, if the null set did not represent or displace itself in the form of the empty set, it could not function within the field of signification or the order of natural numbers.

Another way of putting it with respect to language is that the signifier is not identical to itself because the signifier also belongs to an empty set that contains no signifying elements in it. In the same way the NoF within subjectivity or within neurosis is not really empty and is a foundational stone of the structure although this is not immediately obvious and therefore remains open to negation, refutation, and nullification. The NoF is there as a form of emptiness. But if the NoF is not there as a unary trace, however empty, immaterial, invisible, or abstract it may be, the result, according to Lacan, is a disorder of sense and signification as that found in psychosis.

In neurosis, and so-called normal development, the NoF leads to the negation/primary repression of the mother's narcissistic fantasy about the child, while in psychosis the desire of the mother and its object can lead to the foreclosure of the NoF or the absence of negation and primary repression. The Real and the loss of the object in the image remain unsymbolised and the unified body image is not realised.

In reference to this Lacan asks:

> How does one enter psychosis? How is the subject led, not into alienating himself in the little other, but into becoming this something which, from the field in which nothing can be said, appeals to all the rest, to the field of everything that can be said? (Lacan, 1955–1956, p. 157)

Instead of the normal representation of the desire of the mother and its *objet a* that ordinarily takes place during the mirror phase and with the specular image of the child in the mirror and its symbolic ratification by the NoF, the psychotic subject identifies with the Real thing within the desire of the mother which is fantasised as an imaginary phallus. The imaginary thing/phallus or phantasm mediates the relationship to the object world and to the signifier in perception. The ideal ego in the mirror or later the ego ideal in relationship to the father/ Other both require the prior installation of the NoF and primary repression.

In addition, in *Seminar III* Lacan also considers the effects that the foreclosure of the NoF has on the question of the difference between the sexes. He examines the question of sexual difference in the Freudian cases of Schreber (as an example of psychosis), and Dora (as an example of neurosis).

> In president's Schreber's case this rejected meaning is closely related to primitive bisexuality. In no way has President Schreber ever integrated any type of feminine form. (Lacan, 1955–1956, p. 85)

Primitive bisexuality refers to the early relationship to the mother that both sexes have prior to any sexual difference. Thus Lacan says that Schreber could not integrate any feminine form as something different from him. Instead in his delusion he fantasised being the wife of God and giving birth to a new race. Because of the foreclosure of the NoF, Schreber remained in the position of being the imaginary phallus of the mother, and the lack in the Other was not symbolised in Schreber's mother. Thus, the feminine remained in the phallic position of giving birth to a new race, the father was constructed as omnipotent in the image of God, and castration was rejected in Schreber by acquiring a phallic feminine form. The foreclosure of the NoF is an operation that in this case has two operands: the desire of the mother and the father's imaginary omnipotence as perceived and articulated by both father and son. It is well known that Schreber's father was an authoritarian and cruel pedagogue of the pre-Nazi Era. The omnipotence of Schreber's father is transferred to God that also avoids the question of the phallic function of castration being applied to the father or realising the lack in the Other in the father.

In the case of neurosis,

> When Dora finds herself wondering, "What is a woman?" she is attempting to symbolize the female organ as such. Her identification with the man, bearer of the penis, is for her on this occasion a means of approaching this definition that escapes her. She literally uses the penis an imaginary instrument for apprehending what she hasn't succeeded in symbolizing. (Lacan, 1955–1956, p. 178)

Here Lacan begins to prescient the Real of femininity beyond the phallic order, or what Dora cannot symbolise other than as an imaginary phallus/instrument. Although femininity in the Real requires the prior installation of the NoF, Lacan at times thinks of the Real and of femininity in terms of the foreclosure of symbolisation as in psychosis. Later as we progress with the analysis of *Seminar XXIII* we will see how these two can be differentiated. The Real and femininity can manifest without foreclosure of the NoF. The important thing at this point is that speaking beings (and not only men) have difficulty symbolising the female sexual organ as nothing else but identification with a masculine phallic signifier.

Then for the purposes of understanding psychosis as a disorder of language, he begins to analyse the nature of language itself.

> Let me pause here for a moment so you can appreciate how necessary are the categories of linguistic theory that last year I was trying to make you feel comfortable with. You recall that in linguistics there is the signifier and the signified and that the signifier is to be taken in the sense of the material of language. The trap, the hole that one

must not fall into, is the belief that signifieds are objects, things. The signified is something quite different—it's the meaning, and I explained to you by means of Saint Augustine, who is as much of a linguist as Monsieur Benveniste, that it always refers to meaning, to another meaning. The system of language, at whatever point you take hold of it, never results in an index finger directly indicating a point of reality; it's the whole of reality that is covered by the entire network of language. You can never say that this is what is being designated, for even were you to succeed you would never know what I am designating in this table—for example, the colour, the thickness, the table as object, or whatever else it might be. (Lacan, 1955–1956, p. 32)

You need words to discern this. Discourse has an original property in comparison with pointing. But that is not where we shall find the fundamental reference of discourse. Are we looking for where it stops? Well then, it's always at the level of this problematical term called Being. (Lacan, 1955–1956, p. 137)

What makes the sentence as understood different from the sentence as not understood, is the anticipation of meaning, which in psychiatry is called goal-directed speech: "Discourse is essentially directed at something for which we have no other term than Being" (Lacan, 1955–1956, p. 138).

The question of Being starts prefiguring the question of the signifier in the Real. In this direction, and to try to understand how this takes place in language and in the work of Saussure, Lacan gives the following example from ordinary life.

What link is there between the expression the peace of the evening and what you experience? It's not absurd to ask oneself whether beings [...] could distinguish it from of the other registers under which temporal reality may be apprehended. This might be a panic feeling, for example, over the presence of the world, an agitation you observe at that moment in the behaviour of your cat which appears to be searching left and right for the presence of a ghost, or this anxiety which, although unknown to us, we attribute to primitive peoples over the setting of the sun, when we think that they are perhaps afraid that the sun will not return—which, moreover, isn't unthinkable. In short, a feeling of disquiet, of a quest. There is something here—isn't there?—that leaves intact the question of what the relationship is between this order of being, which has its existence equivalent to all sorts of other existences in our lived experience, and which is called the peace of the evening, and its verbal expression.

What does this being, or not of language, this the peace of the evening mean? And it's precisely insofar as we have been close to it or not aware of it, that we receive it though this peculiar echo phenomenon, which consists in the appearance of what will most commonly be expressed for us by these words, the peace of the evening. We have now come to the limit at which discourse, if it opens onto anything beyond meaning, opens onto the signifier in the real. We shall never know, in the perfect ambiguity in which it dwells, what it owes to this marriage with discourse. (Lacan, 1955–1956, p. 139)

Lacan uses the distinction between a fundamental unconscious language as it appears in delusion and so called-normal language, a beginning of a differentiation between *lalangue* and language.

Throughout the length of Lacan's work, there are three implicit linguistic categories: meaning, signification, and significance (ISR). Sometimes the latter two are collapsed into one, and the translations don't help in this regard. Grigg translates signification as meaning, and significance (*signifiance*) as meaningfulness. Fink translates significance as "signifierness".

Meaning is full and imaginary. Signification is symbolic and refers to the signifier, while significance is empty speech or signification in the sense of meaning without double meaning or too much meaning.

So we find a distinction between signification versus empty formal significance and the full word versus the parrot's empty or idle speech. Already at this point, empty speech has the ambiguity of being idle parrot speech and having purely formal significance that sometimes he calls signification without meaning. In 1953 in *Seminar I* Lacan (1953) spoke of the full speech that he considered true speech regarding desire. However, towards the end of his work (*Seminar XXIV*) the values are reversed and full speech becomes imaginary meaning while the Real of jouissance becomes more closely linked to empty speech. Two different meanings of emptiness are being handled here which are revealed in Lacan's theory of the two holes. In *Seminar III* we already appreciate the ambiguity and bi-valence of the terms that later he will formulate in *Seminar XXIV* as it appears below.

> Full speech is a kind of speech full of meaning. Empty speech is a kind of speech that only has signification. Speech is full of meaning because it starts from duplicity; it's because a word has a "double-meaning" that it is S_2 that the word *meaning* is full of itself. And when I spoke of truth, I was referring to meaning. Signification isn't what people usually thing it is. It's an empty word. It's what is explained in the qualification that Dante placed on his poetry, namely that it be love poetry. Love is nothing but a signification, and we see well how Dante incarnated it. Desire to him, has a meaning, but love—such as I talked about it in my seminar on Ethics, as that which courtly love supports— love is empty. (1976–1977a, session of March 15th, 1977, in the section on "The psychoanalytic swindle")

These different dimensions of language and the signifying chain previously appeared in the graph of desire and are also reflected in how Lacan thinks of the relations among symbolic language, the symbolic unconscious and the descriptive unconscious, and between the Freudian unconscious and repressed speech structured as a language and a cipher. Symbolic language represents the descriptive unconscious that is unconscious but not repressed. When we speak we are not aware of how the structure of language operates within us and determines our experience of the world. The Freudian unconscious in a strict sense is repressed speech, or a more specific form of language within the more general unconscious structure of language. Now *lalangue* is the language of the Real, and is found between the language of desire (the Freudian repressed unconscious) and the language of jouissance (the Lacanian Real unconscious).

In *Seminar III* Lacan refers to what he calls Saussure's schema of the two curves. Lacan is grappling with the definition of the signifier but also with the possibility of how to understand significance or the signifier in the Real. How is it that the signified can also appear as an indefinite cloud or nebula, a mass of feelings, ideas, and sounds, shouts, grunts, which function as signified for the signifier. For Saussure (1915), the signified has two axes: a vertical one composed of air and water (ideas/sounds/feelings) and a horizontal one composed of other signifiers.

The schema of the two curves appears in the course on general linguistics in the section on "Language as organized thought coupled with sound" (Saussure, 1915, p. 111).

Thought apart from words for Saussure is only a shapeless and indistinct mass of ideas and sounds that cannot be differentiated. Differentiated and discrete thought is only possible with language.

> The linguistic fact can therefore be pictured in its totality marked off on both the indefinite plane of jumbled ideas (A) and the equally vague plane of sounds (B). The following diagram gives a rough idea of it:

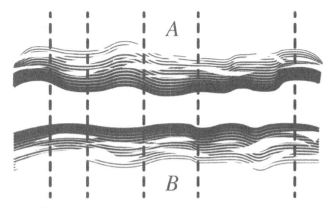

Figure 6. Two curves.

> [...] language works out its units while taking shape
> between two shapeless masses. Visualize the air in con-
> tact with a sheet of water; if the atmospheric pressure
> changes, the surface of the water will be broken up into a
> series of divisions, waves; the waves resemble the union
> or coupling of thought with phonic substance. (Saussure,
> 1915, p. 112)

The vertical lines represent the words that connect ideas to the
sound material.

> Not only are the two domains that are linked by the lin-
> guistic fact shapeless and confused, but the choice of a
> given slice of sound to name a given idea is completely
> arbitrary. (Saussure, 1915, p. 113)

For Saussure the concept or the word is the counterpart of the
mass of feelings, sounds, and ideas; on the other hand, the
sign or the signifier is linked to other interdependent signs/
signifiers within language. So a word can either be substituted
for something in the Real that functions as a signified, or as a

metaphor it can be linked to a chain of signifiers of the same linguistic nature.

For Saussure the signified goes over the signifier, the signified is an amorphous mass of ideas, and the signifier is a sound-image named by the vertical movement of words and which all taken together constitute the sign. Then each unit of the sign represented by a word is linked to every other word.

For Lacan the signifier is intrinsically tied to a word and to phonemes and letters, and ideas and sounds are implicit in the signifier, and the signified is another signifier. For Lacan sounds and images would not be what they are without the signifier, while for Saussure the sound-image has an independent existence from the signifier and is only arbitrarily linked to a word and both constitute the signifier.

To understand psychosis, Lacan renames the plane of thought and the signified as the sentimental mass (a feeling, a shout, a call) carried by the current of discourse, while the signifier is not a sound-image but a disarticulate chain of discourse and a succession of words without meaning or signification.

There is a code shared by a subject and the other, speaking and hearing, a sender and a receiver, S_1 and S_2. When a subject utters a signifier, linked to other signifiers previously uttered, the other simultaneously hears/associates the other signifiers that have been previously uttered by the same subject (in a similar context) and experiences a mass of feelings and sensations (pleasant and unpleasant energetic intensities/ sensitivities) and both of these (the other signifiers or S_2 and the pleasant/unpleasant feelings) function as signifieds for the signifier uttered by a subject.

A signifier is the marriage between code, a name within a battery of signifiers, an idea, and a sound. For Lacan the vertical lines are the quilting points linking together signifier and signified. For Saussure the vertical lines are the words linking ideas to sounds. Words are vertically linked to ideas and sounds and horizontally to other words.

Commentary on sessions 1 and 2
of Lacan's *Seminar XXIII*
Wednesday 18 November 1975 and Wednesday 9 December 1975

Lalangue *and* sinthome

In the session of Wednesday 18th November 1975 Lacan calls
the French language his *lalangue*. *Lalangue*, of course, refers
to the language of the unconscious based on homophony
(words that sound the same), and to the alliterations and oblit-
erations of language that circle around the *objet a* as object of
the drive, and the object cause of desire. *Lalangue* is the language of the One, and how the Real appears within language
and not only in mathematical formalisation or jouissance.

At this point a similar equivocation arises between language
and *lalangue* as between symptom and *sinthome*; both terms
sometimes are used as similar and duplicate and sometimes
as different.

This is an example of the division of one into two appar-
ently identical terms that differentiate: S_1 and S_2. "What is
proper to the signifier, which I called by the name of S_1, is that
there is only one relationship that defines it, the relationship
with S_2: S_1–S_2." (Lacan, session 1 of *Seminar XXIII*). S_1 stands for
lalangue and for *sinthome* while S_2 stands for language and the
symptom.

S_1 without S_2 is undefinable and ambiguous. At the same time
once defined by S_2, there is a remainder of S_1 that remains outside
the categories of S_2. The *act* of speech and the *sound* of speech
remain behind language or the content of speech and what the

27

other hears or understands, although the act and the sound is also heard or has an impact on the body of the receiver. *Lalangue* is associated with the voice and phonation, and the phoneme as an *objet a*, and both say more than the word or the statement.

The relationship between S_1 and S_2 also points to how Lacan's theory has an undefinable or incomprehensible element that cannot be reduced to any theoretical system. It is fine and necessary to have a coherent theory to combine a series of concepts so long as the theory retains an element or dimension that escapes the closure or saturation of the theory. This would be true for both language and mathematics following how Kurt Gödel's theory of incompleteness showed us that the one unifying theory of everything that was promised by mathematics could never be discovered.

A relationship as the word indicates relates/connects two terms but at the same a relationship requires a prior division, separation, and differentiation. The result is a homogenous binary, a dual unity or a duality of oneness, or one dividing into 0 and 1, and 1 and 2. Here 1 is 1 and 0 because 1 has to be 1 and at the same time not 1 (undefined) to become 2. S_2 turns S_1 into something different than the original S_1. S_2 defines S_1, yet the undefined face of S_1 centripetally pulls S_2 back to the S_1 that is both S_1 and S_0. The undefined S_1 that is S_0 refers back to the question of the nebula of the Real that contains jouissance, a mass of contradictory feelings, and undifferentiated ideas and sound images.

So there are two S_1 functioning in two different sets: S_1–S_2 and S_1–S_0. Later on I will use the example of femininity and two types of masters to exemplify the difference between the two S_1.

Lalangue is both S_1 and not the S_1 linked to S_2. In other words *lalangue* is S_1 which equals S_0 or the senseless or without meaning or outside the S_2 of language. S_2 redefines S_1 and turns S_1 into S_2, *lalangue* into language, the signifier into the signified as another signifier. Yet the signified has two meanings, it can either mean another signifier, which establishes a relationship of meaning and signification, or it can mean the use of the signifier to represent significance which represents sounds, the voice as an object, enigmas, and enigmatic affects.

Lacan says that in order to get past S_1–S_2, as the imaginary dimension of the Symbolic, the Borromean knot must be undone. "The knot must come undone. The knot is the only support conceivable for a relation between something and something else" (*Seminar XXIII*, session of 9th December, 1975, p. 9–10). The relation between something and something else, is an S_1–S_2 relation but why is it Imaginary rather than Symbolic? It is imaginary because the dimension of the Real or of the S_1 that is S_0 has been lost and remains as a rogue element within language and the symbolic system. Due to the homogenous binary, the Imaginary has taken the place of the undefined Real in relationship to the Symbolic. The Imaginary appears as a totality of S_1–S_2, when in fact to be grounded in something Real, the Symbolic needs to have a hole where the enigmatic Real may appear. The Symbolic is comprised of at least three elements: 0, 1, and 2. Zero is the third element rather than the number 3 as the product of adding 1+2. When zero is counted as the first unit, then 3 is actually the fourth natural number.

When the knot is undone we go back to the blank drawing board or zero with three or four elements to play with.

Then we start again from the homogenous binary of the Real and the Imaginary, 0 and 1, and the counting of 0 and 1 that makes the first pair of numbers, that is the Symbolic or S_2.

Although 1 comes from zero we don't know about zero until we have 1 and –1. The division of 1 and 0 causes the Real to manifest although the Real already "ex-sisted" rather than pre-existed the 1.

Example

Lacan's says that the French *lalangue* became something different with the injection of Greek, and the word *sinthome* was rendered as symptom. Lacan goes back and names the symptom once again as *sinthome*. In Lacan *lalangue* and *sinthome* fall into the place of the S_1/S_0 or the Real unconscious while language and symptom occupy the place of S_1–S_2, the more usual acceptation of the Freudian unconscious. French is Lacan's *lalangue* rather than language because in this example, he uses *lalangue* to undo the Greek influence on the French language.

In turn for Lacan Joyce Hellenised the English language and said it should be written as *l'elangues*. English or language becomes *lalangue* as a form of jouissance or elation, a luminous hole, a dark or black hole within language.

In the examples of Lacan and Joyce, the French and English languages, one can see how the perspectives are reversible. In French the Greek language and Hellenization can function as S_2 that redefines *sinthome* into symptom, or can function as changing the position that S_1 has in relation to S_2. In the case of Joyce's use of the English language, language becomes *lalangue (elangue)* and symptom also reverts back to *sinthome*, as reflected in the style of his writing.

Elangue becomes elation and elation is not only elation but also *élan* as in *élan* vital or drive, effort, dynamic working, and warmth. But S_1 outside S_2 not only disarticulates S_2 or language by returning language to a form of inarticulate jouissance outside meaning, but also has the potential for rearticulating jouissance, turning a symptom into a *sinthome*, and the jouissance of the Other into the Other jouissance (see the definition of jouissance in Chapter 3).

Lacan then differentiates Nature from Science, or the Real from Nature. Nature is not-one and becomes confused with what is outside nature and belongs to the realm of mathematics. Of course, that mathematics can also be used to prove/probe and affect the structure of nature. Nature and the Real are not-one but not-two either.

The Name and not simply the signifier can be contrasted with the laws of nature. Nomination represents causality in the form of a gap, or the causal in the form of the acausal, as an arbitrary change produced by signification or significance (*signifiance*). Here nomination and the NoF originally associated with the Symbolic, becomes something different operating between the Real and the Symbolic, which Lacan tries to represent through a mathematical topological structure.

With nomination sex becomes nothing natural and is represented by the absence of a sexual relation. Lacan says that in man there is not in him a naturally sexual relationship. Man and woman is not a biological male and female difference, but rather a man and woman in the properly human sense.

Lacan appeals to the biblical myth of Adam and Eve to represent this distinction.

Adam is *Madame (M-adam-e)* and Adam named the beasts in her language and Eve or *l'evie* or the mother of the living immediately used it to speak with the serpent. *Lalangue* is associated with the mother, desire, the mother's desire and the language of desire. One of my analysands told the story that for the last rites for his mother, the rest of the family had tried to exclude him from the ritual. To include him in the ritual his mother had only spoken in her father tongue that only he and his mother could understand and for which he had to serve as her translator for the rest of the group.

Lacan points to the homophony of serpent and *serfesses* in French that means to be afraid or "shit in one's pants"; the serpent is something that causes fear and a misstep.

Obviously here *lalangue* (serpent-*serfesses*) represents something dangerous associated with the object of the drive that needs to be curtailed by the introduction of the symbolic NoF.

The serpent is a flaw, phallus, a misstep, a sin that is the beginning of the *sin-thome*, the first sin, the original sin. We don't know or have knowledge of what the law is without the flaw, and we don't know the flaw without the law.

The sin of eating from the tree of knowledge of good and evil needed to happen for there to be a human world of differentiation, of S_2 and the two emerging from the One. In Paradise there would be no need for knowledge. If you look at the eating of the apple as sin it is a symptom but if you look at it as a structuring gap for the symbolic then it is a *sinthome*.

Original sin or flaw refers to the necessity that the flaw never cease from being written unless the possible cessation produced by symbolic castration intervenes. The flaw never ceases to be written and at the same time as lack it is what ceases to be written by the intervention of repression and the separating effects of the Symbolic.

The flaw or the lack, as the Real within the Symbolic, stimulates the psyche to be continually re-written or to "not stop from being written" and at the same time grants the psyche the opposite characteristic of being under permanent erasure or of cessation or the cessation and obliteration of writing and symbolisation.

Castration begins with an anterior loss of infinite life at the time of birth represented here by the biblical tree of Life. With the tree of knowledge, the tree of Life is lost. The apple represents the tree of knowledge of good and evil, desire and prohibition that divides the tree of unborn life into the experiential knowing of birth and death, pain and joy.

Because there is no discourse that might not be semblance (*Seminar XVIII*, 1970–1971) only a discourse without words can make the impossible possible. The first session of *Seminar XVI* (1968–1969) opens with the claim that the "The essence of psychoanalytic theory is a discourse without words". Similarly, topological figures are meant to articulate those places where speech reaches its limits before the Real. Topology is an example of a discourse without words.

Lacan uses the categories of necessity and the possible from classical modal logic.

In classical modal logic, a proposition is said to be:

1) *possible* if and only if it is *not necessarily false* (regardless of whether it is actually true or actually false);
2) *necessary* if and only if it is *not possibly false*; and
3) *contingent* if and only if it is *not necessarily false* and *not necessarily true* (i.e., possible but not necessarily true).

For those with difficulty with the concept of something being possible but not true, the meaning of these terms may be made more clear by thinking of multiple "possible worlds" (in the sense of Leibniz) or "alternate and parallel universes"; something "necessary" is not possibly false in all possible worlds, something contingent is something where truth or falseness is multivalued and values (of true and false) are distributed according to the context.

Truth as the half-said is incarnated in the signifier S_1 where there must be two of them or two S_1 as already explained. Lacan explains this in terms of femininity. All women are castrated but there is a singularity within each particular woman that is not all under castration. This S_1 of *singular* femininity within the Real is mistaken by the *particular* case whereby all castrated women want to be the one particular "the One woman" who is the phallus and is therefore uncastrated like the master (the One man).

Lacan says *Evie* or the mother of the living tasted the fruit of science and by doing so became no more mortal than or as mortal as Socrates.

Lacan is punning on the status of the singular in Aristotelian logic that did not include it, and only included the particular. As in the syllogism: "All men are mortal. Socrates, is a man, Socrates is mortal."

But then Lacan proceeds to say that *Evie*, or the Hebrew tongue or *Madame* are another name of God and this is why she does not exist (and neither does God—the Real neither is nor is not). Woman, the Real, and God rather "ex-sist". Socrates is also the case of the contingent singular because he accepts to die so that the city may live (not unlike Jesus). Socrates is no longer mortal and becomes contingently immortal as the fountainhead of Western knowledge.

Then Lacan moves on to examine the Greek words *pan* and *me pantes* (the all and the not-all). A woman is not all except as represented by the equivocation in the French *lalangue* "*mais pas ca*", but not that. A woman is not-all in language or in the phallic function. Not-all or not that indicates the place beyond words.

In his seminar ... *ou pire* Lacan (1971–1972) relates "not that" to Wittgenstein's proposition that we should not talk about things for which no words apply. "I ask you to refuse what I am offering you because it's not that". It—is not that. It only looks like It but it is not that. A woman can rarely be the Lacanian version of a Real singular femininity, women commonly revert back to being the particular Freudian "The Woman" who represents the imaginary phallus that both sexes want and lack.

If we cannot say it, then we should not talk about it and pass over it in silence. What one cannot speak "is not that". The only tangible thing about the unsayable, the Real, or the not-all is "it's not that" or alternatively the "Just this" that refers to the singular rather than the particular object, concept, or ordinary name.

The same tangible thing can be said of the *sinthome*: "it's not that." In this respect the *sinthome* that is impossible to pin down to a single definition, is nonetheless a key element of the structure, and what binds the structure together. Lacan in a disarticulate manner will speak of the *sinthome* from different angles and vertex that appear unrelated to the naked eye. First he spoke of the *sinthome* as *lalangue* and then as original sin.

He continues with "woman" as a name of G-d, a name that also has the attribute of not-existing or not being limited to space-time and therefore is a holy ghost or a hollow man like the *"saint-homme"*, who is a *sinthome* madaquin after Adam and Thomas of Aquinas. Woman as a name of God and as *sinthome* transitions into the question of the *sinthome* as "saint-*homme*". Both the jouissance of the mystic and feminine jouissance are "not that" or not-all. Woman is not the phallus and is not all under the phallic function of castration either. Man does not have the phallus because he is under the phallic function of castration but he is not all under castration either because he also has the phallus precisely because he is ruled by the phallic function.

Sinthome madaquin is the *claritas* and consonance of the splendour of Being which is nothing special or has the specialness of the no-thing. The *quidditas* is the "whatness" of an object, the agalma or the *objet a* in the Real. Non-existence as "ex-sistence" is not the opposite of existence, in the same way that emptiness is not the opposite of fullness, and being is not the opposite of non-being. The essence of Being is non-being or non-essence. Emptiness is not an essence because it is beyond attribute or definition. The answer to "what is it", is in the question or the what itself rather than in a world of ideas beyond appearances.

Another quality of the *saint homme* (homophony with *sinthome*) is to be separated from politics. A quality that for Lacan produces *"sint-home rule"* an equivocal term that represents home rule, that government begins at home, sin begins at home or the law begins at home, and also represents the governing of a country by its citizens rather than its elected leaders. Citizens are both individual subjects and also the masses that conservatives fear and view as antinomic to civilisation.

Is this separation from politics equivalent to what Žižek (2005) and others have criticised about French intellectuals who are self-enclosed "in an elitist jargon that precludes the very possibility of functioning as an intellectual engaged in public debates" (p. 105). There are two points that need to be made in this regard. First, is the withdrawal from political life self-imposed or produced by the marginalisation effects of mainstream culture and socially dominant social discourse? Second, Žižek (2005) himself has said that an intellectual or a thinker lives not so much in a world of platonic ideas but rather "ex-sists" outside group identifications. "Ex-sistence" does not represent disregard or being aloof to people or the plight of the oppressed but rather living outside the imaginary struggle for domination.

The space of the subject is found within the lack of the Other or the failure of group identifications and ideologies. This space of the subject within the Other can also be considered a place of cultural and symbolic transformation. Those who use their ego ideals to fight injustice in society, as history has shown, run the risk not so much of getting their hands dirty but of reproducing the very conditions that they are fighting against.

On the other hand, passivity risks leaving the current conditions unchanged and thus the dominant system also benefits from the marginalisation of those that threaten the system from within. As soon as an intellectual, a leader, or writer, acquires enough notoriety the strategy changes and those who are established or the system may increase their attacks or try to co-opt the innovators and assimilate the new insights and inventions to benefit specific interests within the system. Galileo, Newton, Freud, Joyce, and Lacan are all heretics: *heresie*, or RSI (Real, Symbolic, Imaginary).

Heretic is used in the sense of how science questions established authority and tradition and has a particular vertex from which truth may become manifest. In this context, the *sinthome* is now linked to a logical or mathematical approach to the Real. All the heretics mentioned suffered social and academic rejection on account of their work. Their work gave them both pleasure and pain.

Lacan says that something more than being a prick is needed to be a man. This more is the function of the word. Joyce made a name for himself by having others and the university itself read him and interpellate him as Joyce. But this was nomination from the Real more than the symbolic NoF. The latter introduces castration or the castration of the mother-child dyad that represents the child as imaginary phallus of the mother or the mother having an imaginary phallus via the child. The identification with the symbolic NoF inevitably becomes imaginary when it is used to suture or close the gap in the subject left by the castration of the imaginary phallus under primary repression. Nomination or the NoF coming from the Real reopens the gap in the subject in order to introduce the subject of the Real, a process that may involve a significant amount of necessary pain without being masochistic.

Pelagatos is a nobody. An insignificant or mediocre person, without social or economic status.

Here, or a nobody, is a hero and also sounds like the here in heresie. The raising of a poor devil or a nobody to the status of a hero, is how Joyce raised his name and the place of his father. His father was a drunk and a *fenian* which in French means an impostor or fake and lazy man, and also a member of the Sinn Fein movement linked to home rule and to the Irish independence movement from the English.

The artist is the one that speaks the English language in Joycean style. In reading *The Portrait of the Artist as a Young man* Lacan translates young as *comme* in French that also means how (*comment*). So young refers to the adverb "*on ment*" or one lies or a lie is being said, really, mentally, heroically, or in common contemporary adolescent parlance: "that's wicked," "intense", "it's like that". Adolescent talk, is a talk that serious, old, and proper English speaking men hate.

Really in French is *reelment* which Lacan translates as *reelmentant* (the real lying or really lying).

When interpreting one should pay attention to it.

(Ca)qu'ondit—ment (it's just word condiment). Lacan says that in analysis one needs to pay attention to "word condiment".

When all is said and done to *ment* or to mentalize is to lie and the only weapon we have against the *sinthome* is equivocation.

> I sometimes offer myself the luxury of supervising, as it is called, a certain number, a certain number of people who have authorized themselves, in accordance with my formula, to be analysts. There are two stages. There is one stage when they are like the rhinoceros, they do more or less anything and I always approve them. In effect they are always right. The second stage consists in playing with this equivocation which liberate from the symptom. Because it is uniquely by equivocation that interpretation works. There must be something in the signifier that resonates and consonates (consonant-sounds together). (*Seminar XXIII*, session 1, 18th November, 1975)

Resonance and consonance with the Real is what makes accord, *a*-cord, con-cord, a cord or line that is a sound wave and a circle.

Continuing with the seminar of November 18th, Lacan ironically (because this is what they would say about him) calls the English psychoanalysts philosophers because they have a rock solid belief that the word does not have an effect. "They cannot get into their heads that drives are the echo in the body of the fact that there is a saying" (ibid.).

> It is because the body has some orifices of which the most important is the ear, because it cannot be covered (*boucher* is cover but *bouche* is mouth) or closed; it is because of this that there is a response in the body to what I called the voice. (Ibid.)

The ear or the mouth cannot be covered because even if you cover them you cannot perceive without language.

The gaze is an outstanding rival to the ear and the individual presents himself or herself as ruined by the imaginary body that has a power of captivation except in the case of the blind. The blind is not ruined by the body because the body only delivers what Lacan calls the sack or the bubble.

The sack and the bubble are examples of the Imaginary.

For Lacan the notion of consistency is an example of a form that is devoid of meaning. The body has the existence and consistency of a pot or a container. This existence and consistency must be considered real because the Real holds them. The Imaginary shows here its homogeneity to the Real, and that this homogeneity only holds up because of number (concept-*begriff*), in so far as the Imaginary and the Real constitute a binary: one or zero, which is the first pair or the Symbolic S_2.

The sack (Cantor's set, a body, a container) connotes something ambiguous between one and zero. In the external object of visual perception the Imaginary deceives because the image opens the hole of the lack/sack in which we place our own perceptual concepts that constitute the Imaginary. In the example of the "Tusi Illusion", dots that appear to be travelling along straight lines inside a circle, when you take away the straight lines of visual perception, then the dots can be seen as actually travelling in the form of a circle inside a circle. The dots are travelling in the form of a hole that determines the perception of the dots as travelling along straight lines.

This is confusing because ordinarily we are used to think of visual perception as coming from the outside while Lacan is telling us that visual perception comes from the overall knot and that the Imaginary in its homogeneity with the Real simply has the surface of a sack with holes or a bubble with a hole inside its surface. It is in these holes that images are produced when concepts and signifiers are introduced therein.

The consistency of the Imaginary is given by the sack of bones, but also by the hole in the sack and the numbers and letters that are placed in it. All taken together generate a real image that has the consistency of the total Borromean knot.

One of the two S_1 already mentioned is an empty sack and contains nothing and not even zero or the absence of number.

Nevertheless, a null set remains a sack. The Imaginary supports the two of the sack and the hole from the fact that the one is not zero, that the 1 of the trace comes before 0 but that also as unary trace the image does not consist of anything there ({ }). Zero is the first number and one exists thanks to zero (the null set is an inference from the empty set) but at the same time zero does not exist without the one of the unary trace or the 1 image of the null set ({ }).

The pure symbol or image of a set is not yet a concept or a number without the zero concept or number ({0}).

Set of zero (and the null set), set of one, set of two, etc. For Lacan the concept of the set is a third or the sack or a fourth that like the NoF in Lacan was first a symbolic third and then in this seminar the NoF is the fourth of the *sinthome* that comes from the Real. Because one of the two S_1 is the same as zero (and the null set), and zero, one, and two, make three (or four) numbers (including the number that is not a number), then there is no contradiction in saying that the sack is both one of the S_1 as well as the third (or fourth).

There is no intrinsic or constant conjunction between the sack/set and the elements it contains. The sack or the set does not define the contents of the set.

The set is a third because otherwise the empty set would be a no set (the 0 that is not a 0) or a null set rather than a set that has the absence of something in it. The symbol of a set is an image and the symbolic numbers define it. The set is only a concept with the number.

Once numbers are placed inside the Real sack, then the symbol falls back on the Imaginary and the consistency of an image is generated out of the Real sack. The symbol looks different in the Imaginary and evades censorship (even if the symbol does not represent anything repressed or absent) but the value of the Real and the Imaginary are homogenous or equivalent. The duplicate in the pair appears different but it is equivalent, whatever the factual value of the signifier and the signified or S_1–S_2 may be.

The ceiling of the fact or the act of the fact are equivalent and equivocal (*Le fait du fait*). The S_2 stands for the S_1 or is the ceiling or roof for S_1 in the act of enunciation and closes signification upon itself (upon S_2) but by the same token S_1 symbolises S_2 in the act. When I say Rose, I can also say a Rose is a Rose or the image of a Rose which closes or limits the meaning of the Rose or the saying, while two subjects still know a Rose is also a woman or the scent of a woman. A rose can also represent the symbolic act of planting and cultivating roses.

The signified is the arbiter of the meaning of the signifier but in itself does not mean anything (S_0) other than the equivocal meaning of the signifier. The word rose does not mean anything (in particular) other than being the arbiter of whether rose means a flower or a woman but in themselves flower and woman are not arbitrary.

The arbitrary arbiter is the third or master empire/umpire (master of none) that decides on the meaning of S_2.

Finally, the symptom constitutes a neurotic structure while the *sinthome* can represent either psychotic structure or a moment beyond neurosis and psychosis.

The symptom is a metaphor for the loss or the repression of the object/signifier under the symbolic function of the NoF. The symptom can also represent the presence of the lost object and its repression, the presence of the absence or the presence of what was previously lost, fundamentally the archaic mother or the part object of the mother.

The neurotic symptom both reveals the absence of the object and closes the hole with an articulate and interdicting symbolic paternal metaphor. If the loss was caused by accidental and current environmental factors, rather than symbolic factors, then the paternal metaphor will serve to prop up the subject independently from the presence or absence of the current environmental object.

The symptom in psychosis instead appears as a result of:

1) The foreclosure of the cause of repression or the NoF that generates the imaginary and traumatic face of the Real or the apparent absence of the law and its replacement by the rule of the drives and an inconvenient form of jouissance. This is the psychotic disorder itself.

2) The restitutive or curative function of a symptom in a manifest psychosis attempts to close the hole left by the foreclosure of the NoF with an inarticulate language of the jouissance of the Other that speaks between the words but does *not* interdict or pass over the unsayable. The example of this is conveyed by the clinic of delusion.

The *sinthome* also comes in two forms.

In contradistinction to the psychotic symptom, the *sinthome* and the Real NoF appear as a supplement and an addition. Is this different from the restitutive function of a symptom? In other words, is Lacan simply calling the curative function of a symptom a *sinthome*? As later chapters will show the *sinthome* in a psychotic structure has a preventative and reparative function installed at the place where the topological knot of three failed for the subject. In the case of Joyce the *sinthome* exemplified by his writing was installed to prevent the precipitation of a psychotic disorder within what Lacan considered a psychotic structure. In the case of a psychotic disorder the *sinthome* as a fourth element can be used to treat the symptoms of psychosis. The *sinthome* is the virus of the illness that can become the generative letters of a new form of healthy life.

Lacan also uses the NoF coming from the Real, or the *sinthome*, to represent the end of analysis for a neurotic. Lacan spoke of the identification with the *sinthome* instead of with the ego of the analyst (ego psychology) or the good object (object relations) as what marks the end of an analysis. An analysis gradually unfolds as a series of complaints levelled against the other and eventually at the analyst in the transference. The Other is blamed for the symptom. The analysis may be said to end when the symptom is no longer blamed on the Other and the subject can take responsibility for his or her symptom. At this point the symptom becomes a *sinthome* that the subject can identify as his or her own production. This is one simple way to link the concept of identification with the *sinthome* that differs from the identification with the symptom. An analysand felt shame about being identified by the Other as having the marks of past addiction and criminality that only they knew so well. At the same time they felt proud of their symptoms and rejected normative discourse. Their symptoms gave them a street knowledge and jouissance that "normal" people ignore. They felt both proud and ashamed of their identifications. Once they no longer identified with their symptoms this freed them from ego pride and disavowal and shame at the same time. On the other hand, their inside knowledge of addiction and criminality in relationship to the Law are the manure or raw material that will transform the symptom into a *sinthome* or a practical-ethical know-how with regards to the symptom.

The *sinthome* is a formalisation of the language of the One (*lalangue*) that speaks between the words but interdicts the excess of jouissance and meaning and creates a bridge to the Real or the unsayable. The *sinthome* is both a point of impermanence and disequilibrium and a structuring hole for the structure. That the "Father" of the Name is unsayable or is outside meaning is a fact of the structure.

Commentary on sessions 3 and 4 of Lacan's
Seminar XXIII
Wednesday 16 December 1975 and Wednesday 13 January 1976

The untying and tying functions of the Real
The definition of jouissance and the different types of jouissance

Lacan starts out by talking about the seriousness needed for analytic experience whether in sessions or in his seminar. He refers to this seriousness as something "senti-mental" by which he means the feeling or sentiment of an absolute risk, which is one of the ways he will refer to the Real as an experience.

In RSI (1976–1977b) Lacan argues that the Real appears in traces, strokes, or pieces that threaten our imaginary or symbolic sensibilities, the sense or senses through which we understand the world. At the same time those Real points or tips of the Real present the possibility of an absolute consistency rather than the relative consistency represented by the Imaginary.

The consistency of the Real and the Imaginary are homogenous to one another except that ordinarily we only know the consistency of the Imaginary. In visual perception the world appears as a saturated consistent whole. Nevertheless, the consistency of the Real "ex-sists" outside meaning while that of the Imaginary only exists. This "ex-sistence" of the Real with respect to the Imaginary is what lends the Real appearing within the Imaginary the connotation of the uncanny that manifests as a shock, an impact, a knock, or a stroke.

The consistency of the Real is also related to something that is reproduced in the three rings and that makes them equivalent and makes the knot be consistent as an overall knot. Lacan stresses that equivalence is not given by symbolic or imaginary identity. Identity is given by the letters that make the registers different: RSI, or by the different colours (for example, green, red, and black) but the equivalence of the Real is something else: it is an absolute difference, like *das ding*, or the "no-thing". From the point of view of the Real, listening is not listening but hearing, seeing is not seeing but rather insight and realisation, green is not green but the taste that is neither in the tongue nor in the object, red is not red but a cool heat, and black is not black but the non-black in the sense of the uncanny sound or shadow. Finally, last but not least, the sense of smell is not small in importance and the nose knows despite the apparent absence of matter in the air.

Lacan says that the Imaginary and the Symbolic are free from one another and that it is the Real that produces the impact, knot, or needle-point that links them together. Images appear to be independent from words and words appear to be independent of images. People say both things: that an image contains a thousand words, and that a word can generate a thousand images (think of Islamic Calligrams or Egyptian hieroglyphics). The Real limits words and images in two ways: 1. by making them relative to one another; and 2. by presenting an alternative possible or impossible world beyond either one of them. But starting from the moment that the Real ties the other two worlds together, the latter two begin resisting the first. This is the case in the knot of three; in the knot of four it is the *sinthome* or the NoF coming from the Real that ties the knot together.

In session 3 Lacan also introduces a new way of thinking of the subject, and of the subject of the Real in particular. The subject is what is supposed to the fact that the Imaginary and the Symbolic have to support and tolerate the knot of three and what ties them together. The knot is in the process of being tied; the knot is already tied although a subject also participates in the process and is misperceived as the agent of how the Imaginary and the Symbolic are tied together.

In *Seminar XXIII* the Real appears as the maker rather than the disrupter of ties. This is consistent with Lacan defining the Real as "ex-sisting" but also tying the Imaginary and the Symbolic: the Real detains, stops, or arrests them. The Real is responsible for the consistency of the overall knot.

The tie of the Real can be considered as the binding of the drive but the binding of the drive can be considered as either the binding of the Life drive or the Death drive and the fact that these two are also bound together. Both drives have to be considered as having binding and unbinding properties. Sexuality under Eros can make ties between people but can also break them and the death drive can break ties but can also make them in the case of the death drive working for the Law and the Symbolic. The Real as the thing or the archaic *objet a* is the object of the drive while as the organism, it is the source of the drive. But as an absolute difference and as a negative principle, a void, or the no-thing, the Real is the source of the Law in a similar way to Freud's (1920g) use of the Nirvana principle to explain both the drive and the defences against the drives.

Lacan does something similar when he defines the pleasure principle as a limit to enjoyment rather than as the drive for pleasure, the latter being the initial way Freud had conceived of pleasure (the wish to return to an early experience of satisfaction in hallucinatory wish fulfilment, for example). The experience of satisfaction translates to a lowering of tension but the impossibility of returning to a mythical moment of union with the mother's breast, eventually produces a connection between the search for pleasure and an increase of tension.

Instead of the Real being a form of jouissance that needs to be stopped, so that desire can be reached through the inverted ladder of the Law (Lacan, 1960), now the Real has reappeared as the source of the knotting and as the source of the NoF in the form of the *sinthome*. This new form of the Real also requires a new definition of jouissance. The NoF as a *sinthome* is a function of nomination and re-nomination, of knotting and re-knotting. The symbolic law of language and of the signifier is not what binds reality together because the Imaginary will always profess its independence from language; rather it is the Real that binds the two together.

But the homogeneity of the Imaginary and the Real (in visual perception the perceived images appear to make the real world as we see it) in the knot of three also leads to false consistencies since we suppose an ego where the Real makes a tie, and construct a self where there is no self. The paranoid ego is paranoid about the Otherness of the body image. The ego is paranoid about the Real or the empty mirror making a tie between the Other and the ideal ego image. The ego likes to think that the ego or the image in front of the mirror is their own production. Although the case of the ego of the specular image in the mirror (the image of the body, the bodily ego as a surface, and the ideal ego) is a necessary moment and type of alienation (we take the Other for the self) the alienation produced thereof creates a paranoid personality and a normal distortion of vision wherein we think that images come from the outside. The ego is always at risk of being overtaken and its identity destroyed by the Other. Our image comes from the mirror and from the Other. In the mirror phase, the ego appropriates the image from the Other, and from the consistency of the Imaginary the ego projects the ego to the consistency of the entire knot and this is what paranoid psychosis consists of according to Lacan.

Lacan here seems to collapse the distinction between psychotic structure and a psychotic symptom within a neurotic structure. What I was saying about the paranoid structure of the ego and a normal distortion of vision applies to the Borromean knot of three that needs to be undone. In the case of a psychotic structure the Borromean knot of three has not been knotted and needs to be knotted by a structure of four. This is where Lacan says that Joyce's work or *sinthome* seems to meet or coincide with the best results than can be expected from an analysis. The tying of a Borromean knot of four is what the identification with the *sinthome* at the end of analysis and the *sinthome* in Joyce's work have in common. In the case of psychosis the untying of the knot of three is something that has already happened instead of something that could take place in the treatment of neurosis.

The *sinthome*, the Real, and jouissance are concepts that are linked together. The *sinthome* is to the Real and to jouissance what the symptom is to the Symbolic and the signifier. But in Lacan's earlier work, the symbolic screening of the Real, the signifier, and castration were what stopped and refused jouissance in order to generate desire. Now the stopping is being done by the Real in the knot of three and by the *sinthome* emerging from the Real in the knot of four.

The *sinthome* is now linked to transformations of jouissance and the emergence of new nominations and significations. When one form of jouissance is stopped another jouissance is generated or attained. Castration is an indication of jouissance. Lacan's later work posits several types of jouissance and not all of them are malevolent. Phallic jouissance as the second jouissance stops the first jouissance of the Other and the third Other jouissance stops phallic jouissance by not being all under the phallic function of the signifier but still being under the NoF emerging from the Real.

In his lecture at the Catholic University of Louvain in the 1970s Lacan asked his audience whether they could bear the life that they had. From this statement we could say that jouissance points to the impossible experience of bearing the unbearable. In this sense jouissance is intrinsically related to suffering and not just to pleasure or enjoyment or even sexuality as the word commonly refers to in the French language. This conception of jouissance highlights the connection between jouissance and the death drive. In addition, the death drive is not without connections to sexuality since Freud (1920g) also made a distinction between Eros and sexuality: Eros creates bonds and larger unities and sexuality can destroy the same. On the other hand, Freud's theory is paradoxical enough that the death drive working through the Symbolic (defences and the Nirvana principle in Freud's work) and the Real can also generate links, and sexuality as Eros (rather than as a death drive) can also do the same.

It is this paradoxical aspect of the drives and of pain and pleasure that is at the core of the definition of jouissance. The pleasure principle seeks pleasure and the avoidance of pain. When people are asked what gives them the most happiness most respond that their partners are the source of their happiness. Conversely, when they are asked what gives them the most pain (both mental and physical) most answer that loss of love or a loved one is the most painful event. Jouissance seeks satisfaction and in the process it can become suffering and pain when the drive spills over and overruns the defences and barriers that are also generated by the pleasure principle in an attempt to lower or avoid pain. For various reasons, the same object can turn from pleasurable to painful.

This is how in Freud jouissance appears in the symptom as a compromise formation between different psychical agencies. There is the good of pleasure that represents pleasure for the id but pain for the super ego and ego and the pleasure of the good that represents pleasure for the super ego and ego but pain for the id. Pleasure and pain can acquire different meanings and significations within the Imaginary and the Symbolic, but in either case what pleasure and pain have in common is a jouissance that comes from the Real. Thus the transformation of the symptom also involves a transformation of jouissance.

Jouissance is not only malevolent and deadly in a destructive way, as Lacan initially envisioned it, but can also have benevolent aspects as seen in the third jouissance beyond the phallus. What generates this transformation is something internal to the phallic function of castration that both permits and forbids phallic jouissance and causes a movement beyond it. Thanks to symbolic castration and the nomination process associated with the NoF and the capital Phi (as the symbolic phallus), the phallus becomes the signifier of a lack.

In Lacan's early work the inconvenient jouissance is presented in two ways: as a deadly excitation that overcomes the protective barriers set up by the pleasure principle, as a surplus or excess jouissance, and as the malevolent fusion of the mother and the child, when the child occupies the place of the mother's imaginary phallus. The jouissance of the Other between the Real and the Imaginary is an inconvenient jouissance/pleasure because it is impossible to return to the fusion with the mother. The imaginary One with the mother is the Other that does not exist rather than the One that "ex-sists" in the Real (*Il y a de l'Un*—there is something of the One,). There is no Other of the Other because there is no ideal Other, only greater or lesser approximations. The lack in the Other, as the Real within the Symbolic, has to be left open and reconceived. In *Seminar XIX … ou pire* (or worse), Lacan (1971–1972) speaks of the primacy of the One in the register of the Real rather than the Imaginary.

The second jouissance that Lacan discusses in session 3 of *Seminar XXIII* is phallic jouissance. Lacan locates this jouissance between the Symbolic and the Real and links it to the *parletre* or the speaking being and the signifier and to a parasitic form of power. Phallic jouissance is also a surplus or excessive jouissance in that like a foreign organism it threatens to destroy the psychic body with a preoccupation with the bad infinity of the phi as an irrational number. In phallic jouissance there is always a calculation with the power of who has or does not have the phallus. Thus the function of castration and of nomination of the capital Phi as a Name rather than a number is required to put a stop to the parasitic bad infinity of the imaginary phallus.

In *Seminar XIV* on the Logic of the Phantasm, Lacan (1966–1967) developed his use of the golden number (phi and Phi in mathematics) in its relationship to the *objet a* and the phallus. Small phi (0.618 …) represents the imaginary phallus and capital Phi (1.618 …) represents the symbolic phallus and the function of castration. In my last book (Moncayo & Romanowicz, 2015) we develop a formula to represent castration: Phi-phi (1.618–0.618)=1. This 1 would be the One of the Real rather than the Imaginary. Men or women's preoccupation with measuring the size of their breasts or penis, would be an example of the bad infinity of irrational numbers. Phi is an irrational number but naming it and calling it Phi and representing it with a word and symbol puts a stop to the impossibility of defining it with it an exact number (1.68 …).

There has to be a third jouissance beyond the jouissance of the Other and phallic jouissance that would correspond to the new definition of the Real that Lacan is advancing in *Seminar XXIII*. Lacan begun to formulate this third jouissance in his very dense and abstruse paper *La Trosieme* (1975). However, he did not arrive at a clear formulation of the nature of this third jouissance.

The relationship between *lalangue* and jouissance is ambiguous in Lacan. *Lalangue* produces what Lacan calls "Other-jouissance" or "jouissance of the Other". The use of the term Other jouissance is not clear in Lacan's work and often is found confused with the jouissance of the Other. Granted that Lacan, and as Miller and others have pointed out, often was not clear himself about the six or eight names (rather than concepts) he used for the different types of jouissance. Compare, for example, the definitions given in *Seminar XX* and *La Troisième*. In *Seminar XX* there are two jouissances although the concepts used there imply three jouissances.

La Troisième, as the title indicates, is dedicated to the third jouissance by which Lacan mostly means *lalangue* and the jouissance of meaning as a form of the third jouissance. The second jouissance is always phallic jouissance but the first and the third are often confused. The jouissance of the Other refers to the inconvenient drive to be an imaginary One with the mother. The Other jouissance instead refers to the third jouissance that, like feminine jouissance and the jouissance of the mystic (of *Seminar XX*), presumes the existence of phallic jouissance and the intervention of the paternal and symbolic function.

In *Seminar XXIII* he calls it the *jouis-sense* which has been translated as the jouissance of meaning or enjoy-"meant". However, the jouissance of meaning is only one vertex of the third jouissance. The other two being feminine jouissance, and the jouissance of the mystic. These three jouissances are beyond the phallus.

But there are problems associated with reducing the third jouissance to the jouissance of meaning. The first has to do with the word meaning in English given that in French the term is *jouis-sense*. Thus a better translation would have been the jouissance of sense. But sense usually refers to signification and signification is linked to the phallus and this differs from "significance" without sense or meaning. In addition, feminine jouissance and the jouissance of the mystic are linked to the Real, and the jouissance of meaning in this seminar is between the Imaginary and the Symbolic. Meaning for Lacan is more imaginary than symbolic or represents the imaginary face of the Symbolic.

The striving for meaning or goals is linked to a search for purpose, jouissance, pleasure, virtue, or happiness. All of these constitute purposes/intentions of the ego or the ego ideal for success and achievement. Words look for other words, and meaning refers to another meaning, but discourse according to Lacan is fundamentally directed towards Being and circles around a Real of jouissance as a form of lived experience. Ordinarily we would think that discourse stops or ends with the objective reference of discourse. But Lacan stresses that the end of ends is Being although Being cannot be defined with words within language. For this reason, and within language, Being is the same as non-being or non-meaning or senselessness. Being is the hole in discourse, the lack in the Symbolic at the end of a sentence, where words and things, being what they are, could also be something else. This Other within the Other is the Real as a push towards emptiness or the emptiness of Being.

Husserl (1983) distinguished between symbolic representation or linguistic meaning and meaning in the sense of the *noema* or an intention or intentionality associated with a sense that is not representational or linguistic (this is how *sinn* [sense] and *noema* can be distinguished) such as that found in mathematics.

A signifier that in itself or by itself means "no-thing" has to be associated with an intention (that is not another word/signifier) in order to have meaning or sense. *Noema* here is equivalent to mind as intuition but like true intuition it remains abstract or indefinite with respect to its exact meaning within language. I link the *noema*, or a non-linguistic form of intention, to non-thinking or meditative and mathematical thinking. This intention or thought is to be distinguished from both objective social signifiers that represent the subjects of discourse, and from intentions as personal wishes and opinions, prejudice, or idiosyncratic subjectivism.

The noumena or "*nous-men-a*" is the symbolic function of non-thinking or non-goal-directed thinking (thinking without a gaining idea=Nous) which leads the subject towards the *objet a* in the Real. The symbolic function as the function of the cut and of castration vacates or hollows a space or no-space within language where the Real manifests. Thus Nous means both non-thinking and no-sense at the same time. In analysis the ego's search for ideals such as virtue and happiness need to be emptied out from the idealisation, guilt, and paranoia associated with the ego and the super ego. Otherwise, virtue will never be true virtue or happiness, and will remain inextricably tied to vice and suffering. This emptying out takes place when the image of the bodily ego is separated from the object (i/a) and idealisation or narcissism is separated from the Other or from symbolic values (I/A). What remains is a symbolic identification that has been divested of the imaginary trappings that close the gaps within the Symbolic thus blocking access to the Real and to the contradictions within the Symbolic. The holes within the Symbolic are places of non-identification that provide the necessary distance from ideas to transform and evolve the symbolic structure.

A jouissance of the Real within the language of the One, or *lalangue*, is beyond the language of the phallic signifier but is still operative within language. Thus I propose and argue, that phallic jouissance should be placed between the Imaginary and the Symbolic. The aspect of phallic jouissance that needs to be stopped is better identified with small phi or imaginary phallus and the idle speech located between the Imaginary and the Symbolic. Instead the symbolic function and the symbolic phallus can be located between the Symbolic and the Real. This location can also be shared with the third jouissance as the functioning of the void of the Real within the Symbolic and as the intersection between castration or the symbolic phallus (going beyond the phallus) and feminine jouissance and the jouissance of the mystic.

In session 4 Lacan turns to examining the question of *savoir-faire* or "know-how" from the point of view of the artist, the potter, and the artifice or artefact. Know-how is not Techne but rather practice as a Real act or as the Real or the noumena manifesting in activity. Our thinking imputes to God the artifice or artefact that we call the Universe. The Universe means that there is something of the One (*Yadlun* or *Il y a de l'Un*). This One is the Real Other within the Other so that although there is no Other <u>of</u> the Other there is an improbable and impossible Real Other <u>in</u> the Other.

This Real One is not only a jouissance we know nothing of and that manifests as *lalangue* within language, but is also a doing that escapes us. Lacan explains this form of doing with the example of the empty enjoyment or the airy nothing of wit (which has a common association to spirit or *ruach*, a word that also means spirit in Hebrew). The language of the One or of the Real makes sense because it makes no sense. Evolution in nature would be another example of a doing beyond our control. It makes no sense that we come from fish and that gills used for breathing in water became a part not of our respiratory system but of our hearing system. Hearing sounds is a form of breathing, and breathing is a form of "hearing".

The notion of consistency is an example of a form that is empty or devoid of meaning. Consistency represents a surface that holds together. The body is a sack/bag of cloth or a bag of skin holding together bones and organs. But it is enough to see the bag, or the cord of the bag, to recognise the structure of the sack and its contents, yet at the same time the structure and the contents are excluded and not seen. The cord excludes the knot. The knot "ex-sists" and although the cord or the sack appears to exist and the knot does not or "ex-sists", only the knot exists and the Real only exists in the knot.

The speaking being lies about the facts because facts are facts/acts of discourse or speech acts, they are an artifice or artefacts that constitute and determine the subject, nonetheless. The speaking being takes the absolute risk of lying about facts and to say the truth about lying. We speak with the Imaginary or the imagination because the only consistency we know and love is that of the surface of the body.

We mistake the consistency of the Imaginary cord for the consistency of the knot which is how the Real exists and the knot "ex-sists". The only way to say the truth of truth is to follow the traces of the Real or of a Real that consists of the knot and does not exist but in the knot although it also "ex-sists" in the knot and the knot "ex-sists" in the cord or the consistency of imaginary existence.

A knot and the Real are an enigma or E^e (Capital E to the power of small e), a signification without meaning, or significance as he called it in *Seminar III*, a distinction that can be used to distinguish phallic signification from significance without phallic meaning, or any meaning for that matter. This is another reason why the third jouissance has a sense beyond meaning and the senses and constitutes a piece of the Real. An enigma is an enunciation without a statement or a subject of the enunciation without an enunciating ego. Lacan links enigma in this way to writing especially mathematical writing or the use of symbols where letters or pieces of writing have entered the Real and the Imaginary has temporarily ceased or been brought to a stop.

Commentary on sessions 5 and 6 of Lacan's
Seminar XXIII
Wednesday 20 January 1976 and Wednesday 10 February 1976

The name and sexuation
The topology of true and false holes

For session 5 Lacan invites Jacques Aubert to give a presentation at the beginning of the seminar. Aubert was considered an expert on Joyce.

Building on the etymology of the word person in terms of *"personat"* that means to echo and sound through, Aubert reflects on the relationship between person and sound and the sound of the subject: "That or This speaks … "

He comments that in Joyce's writing everything can be understood as a voice-effect through the means of the mask of the person.

He gives the example of the father–son relationship and quotes an exchange from Joyce's Ulysses between Bloom and Rudolph who is supposed to be his father and to have been dead for eighteen years.

Rudolph emerges primarily as a sage or elder of Zion. He has the semblance of a sage of Zion. He feels the semblance of his son with the trembling claws of an old vulture, and speaks like a Jewish elder to the voice within the mask: "What are you doing here, in this place? Have you no soul? Are you not my dear son Leopold, the grandson of Leopold? Are you not my dear son Leopold who left the house of his father and left the god of his fathers Abraham and Jacob?" (Joyce, 1922, p. 416).

And Bloom himself responds:

> "(with precaution): I suppose so. Mosenthal. All that's left
> of him". (Ibid., p. 416)

In Joyce's highly condensed and displaced style, Bloom
responds prudently by saying I suppose so. Immediately after,
Bloom re-introduces the figure of Mosenthal.

The name Mosenthal establishes a connection between the
word of the father and the author of a text that the father had
earlier cited (ibid., p. 73). Mosenthal is the author of a theatre
piece named after a Jewish woman such as Rachel, Deborah,
or Lea, all of which are names of founding matriarchs of the
Jewish tradition.

Bloom confounds the name of the piece, which is the first
name of a woman, with the patronymic (NoF) name of the
author: Mosenthal. In an earlier section of the book Joyce had
written a senseless sentence:

> "What is this the right name is? By M(osenthal) it is. Rachel is
> it? No." (Ibid., p. 73)

Behind the question of the name, what is being articulated is
the suicide of the father eighteen years earlier. Bloom himself
in Joyce's Ulysses is referred to as a renegade Jew, as a Jew
that has joined the opposition. Renegade is also a synonym for
perverted.

Before committing suicide the father had first poisoned the
name by legally changing it through a deed poll or a deed of
trust. In fact, Joyce wrote in his characteristic style that it was
the Name that had poisoned itself, before the father killed himself. The father changed the name to Virag that means "shem-
ale" or *fomme* in French. *Virág* is both a Hungarian feminine
given name and a surname. The name also means flower in

Hungarian like Bloom in English. Virago is also a violent, bad tempered woman.

Again there is a reference here to the Hebrew bible where in Hebrew man is *Ish* and woman *Isha*. Adam names the first woman by adding a letter (a) to the name for a man. A woman is a little bit like a man (plus the a).

All of this material points to how Joyce uses the term epiphany in Stephen Hero. By the term epiphany Joyce meant a spiritual manifestation revealed through the vulgarity of language as a memorable aspect of the spirit. I said earlier in the Preface that:

> Epiphany is a practice of writing or an experience that leaves language unknotted and without a meaning-generating context that leads to comprehension. Nevertheless, incomprehension in time may produce an epiphany or a lantern that opens an easy way into a "non-understanding" that is a form of understanding.

Epiphany is related to a sudden revelation or a manifestation of the Real that at first may appear insignificant or ordinary but the ordinary soon becomes something of a different order (of the Real) revealed in an ordinary experience. Epiphany is a form of jouissance revealed through *lalangue* and the authority of the voice both of which provide a form of experiential certainty and legitimisation not rooted in belief or the grammatical and metaphoric structure of language. Thus, epiphany is associated with the *a* (the voice as an *objet a*) that "M-adam-e" added to ish to create ish*a* or wo-man.

On the other hand, *lalangue* or the language of the Real unconscious is also legitimised by metaphoric and grammatical language, in the same way that a woman is legitimised by a man or masculinity. Conversely, the same way that preconscious language finds its epiphany and legitimisation in *lalangue*, a man is legitimised by a woman or femininity not as a phallic object, but as the *a* found in the sound of the voice.

The topology of false and true holes

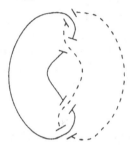

Figure 7. False hole.

In the torus above presented by Lacan, the hole is "false" because the two elements can be isolated without the requirement of a cut. Yet we cannot avoid the fact that they are separate, as there is nothing passing through the middle. In addition, a false hole is artificially created not only by bending and superimposing one circle against the other, but also because the holes within each circle are not continuous with one another.

Therefore, Lacan says that if we include a third element, a line passing through the centre (where the false hole is situated) and through the hole inside the circle, this allows the two to be linked together, and in turn linked to the new line. The addition of an infinite straight line—the equivalent of a circle—to the false hole brings an end to the separation; in its place, now, a triple Borromean knot takes shape, and we have a true hole. We start out with three elements: two circles and a hole. If we count the hole then the straight line would be a fourth element or a knot of four with the *sinthome* as the straight line.

The hole is the equivalent of the Real that ties the knot together and makes the knot exist. But to transform a knot of three to a knot of four, then the straight line passes through the true hole to facilitate a change in the structure.

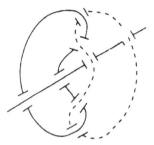

Figure 8. True hole.

Lacan stresses that when the symbol and the symptom (the Symbolic and the Imaginary) are found separate, this is an effect of the discourse of the master. The discourse of the master is precisely that which says: form a circle, in the name of the law. Form a circle out of the two separated circles of the Imaginary and the Symbolic and create a false hole, creating a false articulation between the Symbolic or language and the Real in the form of the imaginary symptom or Ideology that is bound to fall apart or come apart. The discourse of the master becomes undone and needs to become undone like the knot of three. This is an aspect of Lacan's work that may have been influenced by Deleuze and Guattari's (1983) book "Anti-Oedipus" as well as by Foucault's analysis of discourse and power.

Oedipus is a myth of Freud or of psychoanalysis as a manifestation of the discourse of the master, as many critics have argued. However, also consistent with Freud Lacan distinguishes between the discourse of the master and the discourse of the analyst (Lacan, 1969–1970). The master is like the strike of the Real in the knot of three that needs to be replaced by the new invention of the *sinthome* which is the NoF coming from the Real rather than the Symbolic.

The *sinthome* comes from the true hole rather than the false hole associated with the Symbolic or that appears between the Symbolic and the Imaginary or between the symbol and the symptom. In this seminar, Lacan speaks of the false hole and true holes in topological terms. However, these notions were already anticipated in his earlier work in non-topological Freudian terms.

> When the l'esp of a lapse, that is since I can only write in French: when the space of a lapsus no longer carries any meaning (or interpretation), only then is one sure that one is in the unconscious. One *knows*. (Lacan, 1964 [1981], *Seminar XI*, p. vii).

The false hole or the gap in which a lapsus is produced is false, so to speak, because it appears as if there is nothing behind the omission, or the mistake, but the meaning of both is determined by an unconscious repressed signifier that acts as signified or signification for the substitute gap or signifier produced. In the case of a gap or a space that has no meaning, because there is nothing repressed behind it, this is a true hole of the Real unconscious that one "knows" (*savoir*) or experiences but knows (*connaissance*) nothing of it. Knowing in this instance is a form of unknown knowing or a form of knowledge or truth that is not a constituted knowledge.

It is thus no surprise that Lacan uses the invention of the *sinthome* to underscore the properly human aspect of the *sinthome*. To be human requires not only speech but a fall to the ground by which we stand up or that brings us up to a human place or standing position. The notion of artifice as seen in the torus representing the false and true holes is used more in the sense of craft and inventiveness, of something new and surprising from the Real, than artifice in the sense of deception or trickery. Perhaps the false hole is a form of deception but the true hole is a new invention.

> What is specifically human is the act of artifice and this constitutes a new advance, a new conception of what he had proposed before: that the distinctive human characteristic lay in language. Lacan now refers this to invention,

> in terms that certainly necessarily imply language—as
> shown by the order of the symbol—but also another order
> of the knot of four. Let us stress that, for the moment,
> we are dealing with another dimension than that of the
> Symbolic. This already indicates how subversive the
> fourth order may be. (Harari, 1995, p. 88)

Lacan also makes the subtle point of distinguishing between sound or phonation and signification. Ordinarily sound supports the signifier and this would be true for the discourse of the master and the order of language in the knot of three. The sound of the voice of the master creates the knot of three but the sound needs to be disarticulated (the bark without the dog) from the signifier and from the master in order to generate significance. This disarticulation and re-articulation is what is at play in the creation of a new signifier and re-nomination as forms of the *sinthome* and the transformations of the proper name.

Lacan then distinguishes the pleasure that truth produces from the jouissance produced by the Real. This raises the question whether jouissance as a form of the Real is exemplified by masochism or the pleasure of pain and the pain associated with pleasure?

The truth of pleasure and the pleasure of truth as a virtue are not the same thing. Virtue implies the bearing of the unbearable but not pursuing the unbearable; no gain without pain but the gain does not come from the pain or from a "gaining idea"—the truth of the Real is found not sought. To obtain pain out of pleasure or get some pleasure out of pain is not the same as the pleasure that comes from the ethical choice of not calculating the ratio between the cost and benefit of an activity.

How is the true articulated? The answer is that it is found—not sought—and in the form of an entanglement. Here, then, it is not a question of a search for the true, but of "finding" this bit of Real and the jouissance generated in the process.

This is a torus, defined as such by the disk being pierced by a straight or "infinite" line. In other words, the line—whatever its imaginary dimensions—reaches its topological objective by making a hole in the "flat" sphere, and thus making it a torus.

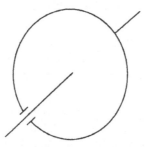

Figure 9. Torus.

The flat sphere would correspond to masochistic receptivity, while the line would stand for the sadistic element passing through that disposition.

For Lacan, Joyce somehow supposed himself to have saved his father. Joyce does this by transforming his unique proper name into a common name that we can all possess and appropriate. However, Lacan argues for a different understanding that distinguishes sadomasochism in this case from the idea of the son submitting to a powerful imaginary father. Although castration is usually understood as the imaginary father symbolically castrating the mother-child dyad and separating them thereby, here castration is on the side of the symbolic father who also presents himself as lacking the phallus, since the phallic symbolic function that the father exercises is, after all, the function of castration that applies to both subject and Other, and the symbolic phallus is a missing phallus.

The father must move beyond the position of the imaginary phallus/father, and this differs from the –phi position of a devalued, contested father. This is a common binary that analysands experience in terms of defining masculinity as either an unbarred, aggressive phallic masculinity, or the masculinity of a father who is a servant or slave to his position *vis-a-vis* his children and wife who are inclined to challenge and contest the father. It is unclear whether the father here represents a –phi in the Imaginary or the way that Phi or the castrated symbolic father is perceived. The symbolic father abandons possession of the imaginary phallus and occupies the place of Phi as the function of castration. He renounces being the absolute imaginary phallus. In doing this, he makes possible symbolic transmission—an act that according to Harari (ibid.) resembles that of the analyst. The analyst also has to reach a position of subjective destitution via his or her own acts and this should not be too quickly labelled as a form of masochism.

Commentary on sessions 7 and 8 of Lacan's *Seminar XXIII*
Wednesday 17 February 1976 and Wednesday 9 March 1976

The proper name and nomination
Topology and the sexual relation

Joyce attributes significance to the proper name (last name) and its transformations. Lacan states that for Joyce a name "can only take place as a nickname", referring to the name "Dedalus" in Joyce's work. Going beyond the S_1 requires the S_2, the nickname or the pen name.

Lacan uses the terms signifier and subject interchangeably. "The signifier is what represents a subject for another signifier" (Lacan, 1961–1962, *Seminar IX*). Mark Twain the writer, for example, is what represents a subject for another signifier (Samuel Clemens). The pen name Mark Twain for Samuel Clemens occupies the place of the Other (S_2) for the subject (S_1). But since Samuel Clemens is representing a subject and is not the subject "itself", the actual subject falls to a Real place "ex-sisting", or non-existing between signifiers.

With the nickname we see the proper name returned to the domain of the ordinary noun. A proper noun is a noun that in its primary application refers to a unique entity. Lacan notes that the proper name must be neither idealised nor devalued but rather reduced to the most ordinary noun. Such a reduction, causes the subject "relief". Harari points out that this refers to the analyst's relief when he manages to dislodge himself, in the analysand's eyes, from the place of "more than S_1", and thus produces a good scenario for the end of analysis. Every proper name was originally a common noun: son of Richard (Richardson), the name Carpenter as indicative of a profession or guild, the name of a mountain, a colour, etc. The Name has to fall from its exalted ego-ideal position, to become something ordinary and out of this ordinary place something splendid may be revealed.

But why does the name have so much significance? According to what Lacan (1961–1962) states in *Seminar IX*, the proper name is not, as Bertrand Russell had claimed, "a word for something particular". The name John originally meant "this" but this can be more than a particular object, it can also be a letter of a singular jouissance. But in either case the name for something particular such as a mountain, a skill, or a colour, and the reference to a singular jouissance or an experience beyond categorical description, are something different than the name signifying an authority or power relationship of domination associated with the NoF or the naming by the father. The NoF in the Real, differs from the patronymic as a signifier of patriarchal domination.

Lacan does not agree with the common assumption that the common noun means something, while the proper name does not. Clinical experience shows many examples where the name means something, the signification linked to a relative, the desire of the Other, a particular destiny, a cultural ideal. Lacan teaches that we have to be especially attentive to the analysand's name and forename, as these are usually bound up with his or her plans, likes and dislikes, choices, moods, opinions, and so on. The proper name is just as important as the common noun: "It is unnecessary to recall how many there are whose activity conforms to their name [...]" (Harari, 1995, p. 158).

Lacan claims that we will understand its function when we have grasped the subjective or emotional response to any alteration of the name. In *Seminar XII* Lacan (1964–1965) situates the essential characteristic of the name in the fact that it is irreplaceable; the name is located in the place of a lack, which it at once suggests and conceals. The name cannot be replaced, because there is no equivalent term in discourse. When a person is addressed by their Name, for example, a person may react with anger when someone gets it wrong, mocks it using vulgar language (an aspect of *lalangue*) or links it to a specific human story or context in which the name was used.

Lacan also emphasises the fact that names cannot be translated (as he puts it, "I am called Lacan in every language"). Whenever one tries to translate a name, this is due to a desire—whether or not one is aware of it—to mock the person being named.

Lacan's own name can be used as an example: *jack lack-an*, lacking jack, empty jack, a subject without substance (S.s.S: "the subject supposed to know" is a *"sujet sans substance"*), which in this case is much more than the signifier itself, since the name as *lalangue* points to a fact of the Real structure of the subject.

Lacan himself gives us another example. At the end of session 6 he says to the audience that he is sure that they have had their fill of him (*votre claque*). "Finally it is over, enough!, he is too much." Let us slap him or clap so that he will stop talking! On his side he also experiences a relief from the fact that it is over, and he got through it, and they can clap for his effort and they can all go home.

Jaclaque Han! Han as a name in Korean and Chinese also means the name of a clan, or the meaning of the name as a group identity or designation. The latter example entails the destination of the analyst's name, its re-entry into the category of the most common noun, becoming the inheritance of a group.

There is an automatism and a *tyche* or surprise in the here and now associated with this event that drives us to mock, or to gather our hands in an act, clap and honour, to bow, to avow or disavow.

This is a case of normal madness or inspiration and that begins with the imposition of the name as a *sinthome* of the imposition of the Other in the Real of speech in the here and now.

Related to this Lacan asks, how can we not all sense that the words that we expect and that we listen to are not in a way imposed on us? Most people dwell in the house created by language and do not complain of being determined by the language they speak or if they do, the complaint is limited to the criticism of conventions or to the critique of those who do not respect the conventions or rules of language or the institutions that control its use. Joyce's sentences are sentences that may violate syntax or the formal rules for constructing sentences in English. His writing rewrites the conventions of language and at first his writing was rejected for violating the rules of syntax as well as the moral code of the culture of his time.

Commonly, the symptom or the complaint about the imposition of language arises around the question of the NoF or the legal imposition of the last name given by the father. In many countries changing the official last name requires a legal act or deed before a judge. Conversely, within Queer, anarchist, or feminist discourses there are those who reject the patronymic as a sign of patriarchal domination. In personal speech the complaint about the name imposed or given by the Other is often observed in the experience of psychoanalysis.

However, even if we get rid of the NoF, without making use of it first, the imposition of language cannot be so easily done away with. Even Joyce who subverted the use of the English language did so while raising his father's name (Joyce) to the status of a new literary invention associated with his name. In addition, when the new generations, choose their own last name (as nowadays youth or groups often do), and then have children, they inevitably pass on the imposition of the name to their offspring. This could not be otherwise, since to not have a name by which to be recognised could be very confusing for small children.

The inevitability of the imposition of the Name seems to mirror the problematic of the master signifier or S_1. There are two master signifiers: The master of the unifying unity or the unary *trait* (i.e., Hitler's moustache standing in for the Nazi ideology) and the master of the unary *trace* or the master of none. The first represents the S_1–S_2 relationship and the second the S_1–S_0 relationship. The first S_1 represents the imaginary phallus (as phi or +phi) and the S_1 in relationship to an ideological struggle for domination or domination through an ideology or a name that reproduces a system, patriarchal or otherwise.

The unary trace or the Name as a process of nomination, as a Name coming from the Real, or the Name as *sinthome*, or the *sinthome* as a Name, is something else or new. The fourth is a third that contains zero, rather than a third as a product of adding 1+2; the 1 in the latter case completes the 2 or the Other of a system or an ideology. The Real in the knot of three is an imposition or a forcing of the Imaginary and the Symbolic into a knot or torus that manifests an antagonistic relationship between the two registers of the Imaginary and the Symbolic, and the Real is also mistaken for one or the other. Either images supersede and hide the code that builds them, or words eliminate and deconstruct the realism provided by images. With the knot of four, each register can keep its independent contribution and at the same time be in a relationship of interdependency to each other. The Real can remain unnameable and unknowable and at the same time be named and used for constructive purposes.

Words determine us and are themselves determined by the symbolic structure, which is itself determined by a mathematical structure, that itself is determined by an undetermined and indefinable exterior Real. We find two levels of determination and one of indetermination, therefore. But something of the exterior Real outside the boundary of the known universe passes into the interior Real that is part of the topological knot and of the structure of language. The Real lives or "ex-sists" within the Symbolic in the form of *lalangue* or the language of the One that appears in the holes of the symbolic structure.

The sick person sometimes instead of being a person who is not normal or well can be somebody who overtly suffers from the common illnesses that so-called normal people do not realise that they have. Lacan says "Why doesn't a normal person know that the word is a form of cancer/virus with which the human being is afflicted."

In Joyce the written language is so imposed on him that in the end he finishes by dissolving language itself. The structure of language determines him and in the end, and out of the indeterminate and undetermined Real, he ends up determining the structure of language. It is through writing that the word is decomposed in its function of imposing itself.

For Lacan it is a matter of liberating oneself from the parasite (a symbiotic type of relationship where one benefits and the other is harmed) of the word (i.e., as in the malevolent example of *lalangue* within language represented by clanging associations in psychosis) or, to the contrary, a question of allowing oneself to be invaded by the constructive phonemic and polyphonic properties of the word (i.e., benevolent *lalangue* within poetic speech or language).

According to Lacan a Freudian slip is an error in the structure of the knot where the cord fails to go under or above another cord creating thereby an entanglement between a mistake, an error, and a transgression.

The paternal lack, the lack in the father, or the lack of a father, creates an error in the knot that requires the *sinthome* as a supplement or suppletion to knot the structure back together.

In relationship to this point about the error in the Name/ knot or the paternal lack one may ask following Lacan (1956–1957): "Which register of the lack is the seminar invoking"? The lack in the real father, the symbolic NoF, or the imaginary father, the important and hated or contested father of the family romance? The father has desire for the mother, the father is under the NoF, and the imaginary obfuscates the unary or unmarked aspect of the NoF as if it did not exist or conversely turns a unary trait into a grandiose master signifier. This is the confusion that reigns regarding the so-called weak family fathers and the corresponding vindications that are used to explain all sorts of social and psychical disorders.

The symbolic father is a castrated father given that the symbolic phallus is a missing phallus. The father is also under the phallic function of castration. But this may be misunderstood and apprehended in an imaginary sense as a weakness or defect, as an imaginary form of castration, when in fact symbolic castration facilitates phallic jouissance. In addition, the symbolic father is also in the place of the lack in the Other or the barred Other. As we have seen the barred Other is also a symbol for the null set ($\emptyset$). The null set and the NoF emerging from the Real manifest in the Borromean knot at the place of intersection of the Symbolic and the Real. The NoF in relationship to the Real functions like the null set and the unary trace that have the quality of nullification and emptiness. This also can be confused with weakness or absence when in fact the NoF coming from the Real is an undefinable presence, an S_1 as a singularity that is not part of an S_1–S_2 chain.

The problem is further complicated by the fact that the family father is not the same as the Real father that in Lacan refers to the father's desire for the mother, although both could be true in the case of Joyce. In addition, the biological father is not the symbolic father who recognises and raises the child. When speaking of the foreclosure of the NoF in psychosis we are primarily referring to the NoF in its primary repressive symbolic function.

In ordinary circumstances and in ordinary neurosis the NoF represses or writes its speech on the question of the child being the imaginary phallus of the mother. The repression of the imaginary phallus creates a gap in the subject, which then the Name will also offer to close with the imaginary function of the Name. John Joyce did not play this imaginary function for Joyce but many fathers don't either. This is what lies behind the desire to vindicate the father and the desire to be famous and make the name famous. This is not primarily an indication of psychosis or a compensation for psychosis—it can be a moment of ordinary madness; either an aspect of the illness or of the solution to the illness.

Joyce may have needed to make a name for himself and build himself an imaginary ego to neurotise his psychotic structure. In the case of a writer with a neurotic structure the opposite could have been the case. In the Oxfordian theory of Shakespeare's authorship, that Freud (1930e, 1940a [1938]) endorsed, Shakespeare was really the Earl of Oxford Edward de Vere who was in potential line of succession to the crown and needed to keep his writings anonymous. De Vere used Shakespeare as a ghost writer to "shake his spear". At the time, a noble man was expected to be a warrior, governor, and landlord but not a writer that could expose the internal drama and power machinery of the monarchy. The Earl of Oxford used Shakespeare as a pseudonym to become an ordinary noun and protect the legacy of his work. His relinquishing of his Name was an effect of nomination that transformed the name of Shakespeare into a Real name or the NoF emerging out of the Real.

The imaginary function of the name appears as a compromise formation between the symbolic name and the symbolic castration of the child as imaginary phallus of the mother. The symbolic name is replaced by the imaginary name and the imaginary name also replaces the phallus, the mother, and the child, thus deriving its potentiated power and intensity.

But the imaginary use of the Name generates an unstable order or a leaky plug, a house of cards, a structure held together with tooth picks as in the case of the paranoid ego that is always at risk of being revealed as lacking and falling apart. The subject is constituted or imposed a subjectivity by the name, but when the subject identifies with the imaginary name to close the gap left in the subject by the symbolic name and the establishment of subjectivity, this appropriation is unstable given that in this case the name and the narcissistic investment of the name is always threatened by lack. Thus the imposition of the symbolic Name and the imaginary use of the Name as an imaginary identification still requires a nominating process by which a name becomes an ordinary noun in circulation among and uttered by others other than the subject. The signifier now represents a subject that may or may not be there or may have vanished or disappeared.

This is the enigmatic Name that comes out of the Real. But is this really the enigmatic Name that comes from the Real or does this way of talking about the Name represent the mystified and reified metaphysical talk about Being or Life that materialists reject? Is this simply a way to legitimise, obfuscate, and obscure the rampant theme of the struggle for power and historical domination, and the hegemony associated with patriarchy, phallocentrism, and the S_1 of the master and the imaginary phallus?

Nomination, for example, is used to nominate or appoint someone to a political office, or to an award like the Hollywood Oscars, or the Nobel prize. All of these are associated with the politics of knowledge, stardom/fame, and varied economic interests. Joyce, Freud, and Lacan, were all concerned with fame and having their name linked to history and posterity. In this sense, nomination is very much associated, not only with the name being used by and circulated by the Other, but also, and perhaps more importantly, with the narcissism and ego ideal (values, ideas, identifications) of the subject. It is the latter, which is accepted and considered inevitable by people of all sorts of persuasions, that is inextricably involved with the imaginary phallus and the question of domination. The question of making a name for oneself can also be associated with the imaginary function of the Name that serves as a stop-gap for the lack in the subject.

Materialists critique domination and at the same time are very much involved in the historical struggle for power and domination which eventually may end up proven wrong by history itself or the law of unintended consequences. The political struggle to replace the master eventually simply produces a change of masters but does not replace or transform the discourse of the master. Materialism becomes materialistic or simply a renewed face of the master's discourse. Both patriarchy/male chauvinism and matriarchy or feminism, capitalism and socialism, become forms of the master's discourse. What is at stake in recognising the two forms of S_1 goes beyond simply recognising that the attempt at emancipation always fails and is always revealed as a renewed form of hegemony or domination.

Both idealism or mystification, and materialism, can be ways of misrecognising what is really at stake in the process of nomination and the nature of power. The misrecognition is given by not recognising the void nature of the Real. The NoF represents the gift and the debt associated with bearing the ordeal of symbolic castration. This is the negative power of the symbolic phallus associated with the lack in the Other, or the Real manifesting within the Symbolic. Now making a name for oneself means both appropriating the NoF, and bearing the symbolic castration associated with it, and not using the Name to cover the lack but rather to reveal it (in the form of the common noun).

The Name that comes from the Real of jouissance (a singularity rather than a particular object or concept) is also linked to the Real of an ethical practice. Ethical here is not defined by a reward or result within a moral code, but by the doing of an activity or a true practice without a consideration of a result, the merit, or the power associated with an office or position within a hierarchical structure or meritocracy. Typically, the moral or the meritorious and the ethical cannot be clearly differentiated and thus the master's discourse and the analytical discourse, or the two master signifiers (master of a system and master of none) are often confused. However, revolutionary changes and evolutions of the Other or the symbolic structure are the result of true ethical practices that involve ordeals and pain and conflicts with the Other that are not masochistically chosen as ends in themselves or are not meant to sadistically destroy the humanity or the fantasised completeness of the Other. The subject as a hole in the Other, already knows that the Other is lacking or empty.

The ego (small i) has to be separated from the object (i/a) and the capital I (for the ego ideal) has to be separated from the A or O. What is this small i without the a, and the a without the imaginary i? What is the I without A or the A without I? The i associated with the a, produces an artificial form of intelligence (a/i), while the a separated from the i, produces a properly human form of knowing, or unknown-knowing. The ego without the object is what transforms the subject of narcissism, or a sense of wholeness and consistency associated with the known universe of facts, and the lack in the Other constitutes a new place for the subject. Ideals without fixed ideas, ideas without Ideals, or thoughts based on non-thoughts.

But non-thoughts are inseparable from thoughts and ideals are inseparable from ideas so where does this leave us? We are left with thoughts that have spaces in between like planets or particles that are both particle and waves within energetic fields.

We are left with images of both objects and their shadows. The shadows are comprised within the images in such a way that the dimensions of the image can be written or inscribed within them. It is not unlike writing a computer code for a telescope comprised of a hole and a mirror that registers images of the outer universe.

The Real is the light, the hole, and the mirror. The Imaginary are the images. The code is the Symbolic. The Borromean knot can be alternatively conceived as the imagination, the process of Nomination, and the space/field all around that rewinds and nullifies ($\emptyset$) the entire enterprise. The Imagination supersedes the process of symbolisation and formalisation, and the process of Nomination supersedes the objects of the Imaginary.

The *objet a* as the affective and intensive representative of unborn life or the heart of knowing and *lalangue*, rather than go into the S_1 of the imaginary phallus (the signified of the repressive symbolic function of the NoF or S_2), can become a numerator of S_2 or the NoF as a unary trace of the Real or of the Real within the Symbolic. In the formula for the discourse of the analyst the *objet a* in the Real becomes a numerator of S_2 or the NoF as unary a trace of the Real or of the Real within the Symbolic.

S_1/S_2 has symbolic equivalence with S_0 or the *objet a* in the Real. The *objet a* represents the interior Real within the knot and is a semblance of being or unbeing or the being of emptiness. The *objet a* represents the null set of Infinite Life without a name, concept or number. The latter is the exterior Real outside the knot, and the *objet a* is a semblance of the interior Real inside the knot, the hole on the surface or inside the structure through which lights travel to make the images of the Imaginary.

Lacan also says that the slip or the error in the structure is what grounds the notion of the unconscious. It also makes a difference at which crossing point between the lines of the knot is the slip corrected. The slip has different consequences depending on the place of the knot where it happens. The slippage is repaired with a *sinthome*.

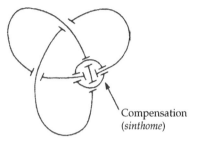

Compensation
(*sinthome*)

Figure 10. *Sinthome*.

A slip or mistake has the structure of a symptom due to repression. A metaphor or symbol appears in the place of something that has been repressed. The symptom according to Freud is a compromise formation between repressed and repressive unconscious forces. But since the symptom requires repression and primary repression is missing in psychosis, the repressed in psychosis appears differently without articulation. There is also in Freud a difference between two aspects of the symptom in clinical psychosis. Thought disorder is the primary manifestation of the disorder, while delusion represents its restitutive function or an organic attempt at curing or defending against the disorder. From this perspective, the question arises whether these two aspects of the symptom parallel a difference between symptom and *sinthome* or whether the reparative function in both cases is substantially different.

The psychotic symptom reveals a disarticulation of language and a failed attempt at articulation in delusion. The *sinthome* instead is an attempt to repair the damage in the primary repression or the paternal metaphor that caused the primary symptom of thought disorder. Directed by the NoF coming from the Real and the benevolent language of the One or *lalangue*, rather than the symptom of delusion, the *sinthome* repairs the lack or failure of symbolic metaphor by an effect of Nomination across the Imaginary and Real registers.

If the symptom is metaphorical, by contrast nomination does not work according to a pattern of substitution: it is not a replacement of anything else, but sets itself up for and by itself at the site of reparation where the "slip" or failure has occurred. Metaphor remains within the order of the signifier, while Nomination works by means of the letter.

The distinction between symptom and *sinthome* is coextensive to the difference between the Lacan of the Symbolic and the Lacan of the Real and jouissance. The symptom is no longer a metaphor but a form of jouissance that cannot be easily removed with an interpretation (such as a medicine given to a patient) but instead requires an intervention somewhat akin to surgery that introduces cuts and artificial organs, pace makers, electrodes, etc. The repairs to the knot in the form of the *sinthome* are interventions and cuts to repair failures in the psyche.

In psychosis, the *sinthome* occurs at a difference place of the knot that preserves the links between the Symbolic and the Real found in the knot of three. But in the knot of four in neurosis, since primary repression has already been installed, what happens differently from psychoses is that primary repression and repression acquire a different enigmatic signification. In the neurotic knot of four repression or the NoF includes the true hole of the null set that in the end is no repression of meaning at all but simply the emptiness of signification and of desire.

A symptom may or may not be permanently eradicated. People often wonder whether people change or not, and whether psychotherapy or medications, can cure symptoms, and if they do, they may do so only temporarily or episodically. In addition, this problem is also applied to the question of character. Does character change or is it permanently fixed? Often clinicians blame the difficulty involved in removing the symptom to the fact that a symptom is rooted in a characterological structure or trait. The person may be willing to collaborate and wish to cure a symptom but if it is rooted in a character trait this is something they identify with and do not want to change. The symptom may be ego-dystonic but the character trait is ego syntonic.

The concept of *sinthome* implies that the symptom is a form of jouissance rather than a metaphor, and this explains its imperviousness to change, and to change as a result of interpretation or explanation. The symptom causes pain for the ego or is something bad the ego wants to change but at the same time remains rooted in something positive or pleasurable that the ego also identifies with. The bad may be good, and the good may be bad. The bad in the symptom and the pleasurable in character need to be resignified but this may not mean the end of the symptom. Rather, a new relationship to the symptom will be established and this is what Lacan means by the subject becoming a disciple of the symptom. This change will continue to produce post-analytic effects after the end of treatment or analysis. Instead of being identified with traits that reinforce symptoms, the subject will now be identified with the *sinthome* rather than the ego or the *sinthome* will become a new form of the ego that ties the Real and the Symbolic together. This new awareness of the *sinthome* or this new ego acquires the capability of symbolising and bearing the experience of jouissance, knowing, and *lalangue* emerging from the Real unconscious.

Topology and the sexual relation

In this seminar Lacan will use topology to explain what he had already called (1972–1973) the absence of the sexual relation between the sexes.

He points to the equivalence of the internal eight and the circle in the middle because without the repair they are both circles. The circle in the middle can become an eight or the eight can become a circle. All you have to do to turn a circle into an eight is to fold the right side of the circle over its left side.

Figure 11. Sexual relation 1.

Figure 12. Sexual relation 2.

Figure 13. Circle and eight.

But in this equivalence between the two circles there is no relationship because they are separate parts that do not make a knot through which both need each other to exist in their individuality. The failure of the knot is equivalent in both sexes. So both sexes are equivalent, they are both circles.

It is clear in Lacan's text that when there is equivalence between the sexes there is no interdependent relationship. It is also clear that when the failure of the knot is repaired with a symptom then the two sexes are no longer equivalent and now there is a relationship. So equivalence=no relationship, and no equivalence=relationship. But what does this relationship or no relationship have to do with the absence or presence of a sexual relation? Does Lacan mean the same thing by relationship and sexual relation? In addition, does he mean the same thing by symptom and *sinthome* in this instance? One is duplicated into two, and then when the second is again sub-divided into two then we have three, but is the third here a symptom that creates a knot or a *sinthome* since the *sinthome* is a fourth element?

Sinthome points to a repair so that there can be a relationship but by the same token once there is a relationship the symp-tom impedes the sexual relation or makes for the absence of a sexual relation and for neurosis within a relationship. Absence of sexual relation does not mean that couples don't have sex. Symptom here means each sex is relating to their own narcis-sistic object in the sexual relation so there is no sexual relation to the other as such. The other functions as a symptom of the subject as what impedes/facilitates the sexual act and/or a relationship or what remains in the form of the memories asso-ciated with the other: the caresses, the words, the environment, or the pleasure thereof. So there is a sexual act facilitated by the relationship and at the same time there is no relation. Thus an interesting paradox is produced between *sinthome* and symp-tom. *Sinthome* repairs and symptom damages or injures either in the form of pain or in the form of pleasure turned into pain.

If the failure of relationship is repaired (by knotting the middle circle into the eight or the two circles) with the symp-tom in the same place where the failure is (in the middle in the example above), the sexes are no longer equivalent because one is still a circle (the one that repairs) and the other becomes a knot. They are both circles that lock each other because the middle circle prevents the internal eight from becoming a circle once again.

Now there is no equivalence so there is a relationship and because there is a symptom/*sinthome* a couple has sex although this also means there is no sexual relation. For there to be a relationship there has to be a symptom/*sinthome* but by the same token if the symptom exists not only then there is no sexual relation but there is neurosis as well. Either in equivalence or non-equivalence there is no sexual relation. Non-equivalence and the symptom seem to be the pre-condition of a relationship and the sexual act but equivalence within non-equivalence seems to continue in the lack of sexual rapport between the sexes. Both sexes have in common that in the sexual act they are both relating to their own object rather than the other. If there is a relationship then the symptom, the sexual act, and the lack of a sexual relation all arise together.

How does this logical and topological problem of the symptom in relationships appear in the practice of analysis and the relationships between the sexes? Freud was cognisant that relationships are vulnerable to the split between tenderness or love without sex or sex without tenderness and love. Speaking beings are prone to desire those they don't love or don't depend on and love and care or depend on those they don't desire. This state of affairs explains many unhappy marriages or unions and infidelities within married or coupled life.

Now one could also point to the developmental norm where love and genital sex can be fused under the phallic phase and the law of conventional marriage. However, people and youth nowadays reject this normative ideal as oppressive or heteronormative, and the reality is that this fusion or stability in relationships as well as love and sex are impermanent and does not lead to a stable sexual relationship. Freud who was married all his life at a time when the institution of marriage was still strong in Western culture, and Lacan who had several long-term and short-term relationships and a traditional marriage, were brutally realistic and "objective" about relationships and were not prone to humanistic and idealistic views or romantic fantasies about relationships.

Let me provide you with a quick sample of symptomatic relationships from the contemporary practice of analysis or from descriptions of neurotic symptoms in terms of relationship problems that demonstrate the absence of a sexual relation in the Lacanian sense. Laura who is a successful professional woman cannot tolerate the lack or shortcomings in her partners. She feels humiliated by men and in turn attacks them, rejects them or leaves them for other men or for what she does not like about them. The humiliation she experiences may come from critical comments of the other or from the relationship to the capital Phi function of symbolic castration that women experience in relationship to men. At least three relationships in her life fitted this pattern. Tina does not know whether she wants to be in a relationship or not and feels hurt by the needs and demands she places on the other or on a man who does not know whether he wants to be with her because of what his family may think of her as his partner, or otherwise. However, being in the early phase of their relationship they have a satisfying sexual relation in the sense of the sexual act.

Thomas wants to be in the relationship he has but feels trapped and controlled by his partner which leads him to want to be with somebody else or another partner. Peter's partner wants to get married and have kids and he doesn't want to get married and have kids but doesn't want to lose her and so they are at an impasse. Or Mary who did not want to be with her partner and rejected him but does not want to be alone and this pattern has repeated itself her entire life. Martha gets involved in sado-masochistic relationships with men and is fixated on being hit in sex but wants to marry a "normal" man and have a family. Charles gets involved with men that abuse him and is interested in pornography but wants to have a loving lasting relationship with a man he cannot find. Another man is involved with a woman who is a maternal figure and with whom he does not have sex but doesn't want to leave her and goes to massage parlours for sex. Finally a young woman is with a man who loves her and wants a family with her but she doesn't want to have any more kids because she left her two kids and their fathers behind.

Lacan says that the *sinthome* is the sex to which I do not belong. A woman is a symptom for a man. Is a man a *sinthome* for a woman if *sinthome* is non-equivalence? Lacan answers saying anything you please, an affliction, a devastation.

Lacan at this point uses symptom and *sinthome* interchangeably. Lacan's formulation of the absence of harmony between the sexes in the sexual relation is nothing new and follows from Freud's ideas. Both sexes are objects of fantasy to each other, which interferes with the maintenance of an intimate rapport between the masculine and the feminine. In their sexual relation they don't see the other as another subject, but as who the object is in their own fantasy. A woman is a symptom for a man of what he lacks to be complete due to the incompleteness and the loss linked to symbolic castration. A woman is the phallus for a man, and a man has the phallus that a woman lacks and wants.

Eventually we know that this formula is bound to fail, and that the only ties that may remain are those associated with symbolic commitments which not everyone will choose or prefer. Now Lacan is raising this question in the context of the *sinthome*. Since the sexual relation will both succeed and fail, this can lead to an endless search for the object that will also eventually fail, or the alternate strategy of staying in a relationship past the point of realising the absence of a sexual relation. Either choice has gains and losses associated with it. If both symptom and *sinthome* are the same then the repair associated with the *sinthome* is a temporary repair at best that makes a neurotic relationship possible, that sooner or later will also fail.

In the case of psychosis we showed how symptom and *sinthome* are different. The symptom either disarticulates (loose associations) or rearticulates (delusion) the signifier in such a way that the links between the Symbolic and Real fail and only the Imaginary prevails in its independence from these two. The *sinthome* holds the promise of tying the three together although the Imaginary remains untied otherwise. The symptom manifests a restitutive function in a delusion when it attempts to relink the associations although the tear in the net of signifiers remains unchanged. The delusion still fails at critical points of the net. The reparative function of the *sinthome* is different in that given the effects of nomination, the Imaginary although still loose by itself, can be re-knotted thanks to the cord of the *sinthome*.

Another way of thinking of the difference between the two is that the *sinthome* is the constructive or revelatory aspect of the symptom, the part of the symptom or of the pain associated with the symptom that precipitates evolution, and a repositioning of the registers. The subject is a disciple of the symptom, as Lacan has stated, and this could serve as another definition of the *sinthome*. In neurosis, and in a formal definition of the end of analysis, the registers are unknotted, and then re-knotted once again through the *sinthome*. There may be pain but the pain serves a purpose beyond simply pleasure or masochism. Frustration and symbolic castration could serve as examples of pain with a purpose.

Phi as the phallic function of castration, appears in the place of the lack in the Other, which means that the lack may produce an imaginary substitute, but may also result in the square root of minus one which is a signifier without a signified. This signifier or Name produces something unpronounceable as a residue or Real bit. The effect of using the NoF that comes out of the Real is its disappearance as an external imposition that results in a repositioning of the subject in relationship to the Real. This is another way to differentiate symptom from *sinthome*.

In this sense a man for a woman, or masculinity for femininity cannot merely represent an affliction or devastation although this could also be at play. A fantasy can sustain desire or compensate for castration as in the case of the woman symptom for a man but can also defend against or invoke castration. The latter would be the man symptom for a woman. The man-symptom for a woman helps her defend against castration or invokes it. The man symptom for a woman is the man that is perceived as having the phallus that she does not have and a man who is a provider and sometimes a source of identifications.

But a man as a *sinthome* for a woman also provides access to capital Phi or the function of castration and of the Name which then facilitates access to the Real of femininity or the square root of minus one. *Sinthome* for a woman would be the devastation or the subjective destitution of the capital Phi and the Real of femininity. The Phi of the phallic function of castration gives access to phallic jouissance and at the same time to something beyond the phallus since the symbolic phallus is missing and is found in the place of the lack in the Other. The signifier of a lack goes into the lack of a signifier associated with femininity and feminine jouissance. Jouissance here raises the question of who am I and does the woman exist. The woman does not exist in the sense that a hysterical woman can go from love to desperate pleas, to cruel virago, derision, and rejection. There is no subject behind these masks that can address the contradiction between the two positions. This is one meaning of the woman does not exist for the woman is trapped here in the vicissitudes of the phi and –phi associated with the imaginary phallus and imaginary femininity and masculinity. But in relationship to the Real a woman "ex-sists" and this opens the question of an access to a different form of jouissance and knowledge in and of the Real made possible by the Phi of the phallic function of castration. The *sinthome* as subjective destitution for a woman holds the possibility of a different category of femininity beyond the phallic order.

In contrast the man symptom for a woman is when the relationship to having the phallus is through the man who has it or has the +small phi or does not have it and represents –phi, a common dynamic of relationships. In either case the positive or negative manifestations here are mostly imaginary.

Is there a difference in how a woman is a symptom or *sinthome* for a man? *The* woman as symptom is a woman who becomes the object of a man's lack and desire. He is beside himself without her and fervently desires her. This is the woman that needs to be relinquished or let go. A woman as *sinthome* may allow for some degree of repair instead of simply ravishing a man with jouissance. When a woman functions as *sinthome* for a man he may come to terms with his own lack and abandon the fantasy that he can be complete only in her presence. Accepting his own castration may lead to the possibility of a different form of relationship and jouissance.

Let us recapitulate the difference between sexual relation, sexual act, and relationship. Symptom is linked to no sexual relation but facilitates the sexual act and puts the relationship at odds. There is no sexual relation because phallic jouissance or the sexual act is with an object of fantasy which benefits only one or both in different ways. The object of fantasy is triggered by imaginary partial signifiers of the other such as clothes, cars, body parts, knowledge, money, voice, smell, etc. The absence of a sexual relation can lead to the presence or absence of the sexual act. A woman may refuse or accede to sex due to feeling devalued or devaluing herself with a man/symptom and a man may be impotent when faced with his woman/symptom or through the act of sex may construe the woman into a symptom.

As distinguished from the sexual relation, or the sexual act, a relationship could be defined not as the presence of the sexual act or the absence of a sexual relation in the technical sense meant by Lacan but as the maintenance of a link through the *sinthome* in non-equivalence between the sexes. Finally, the absence of a sexual relation can occur with or without the sexual act. Let us now consider to what extent the relationship between Joyce and Nora can shed some lights on these questions.

Joyce and Nora

For Lacan only in the example of Joyce for whom his wife is neither symptom nor *sinthome* was there a sexual relation with his woman, a sexual act, and a relationship. The sexual relation with his object woman was not phallic. Yet the facts of their relationship show that although she was not the phallus for him she had the imaginary phallus in terms of the *objet a* primarily in the form of the anal object. They had a sexual relation and a relationship, she was the only woman for him and he degraded, debased, or depreciated her. Is this the same as perversion?

Joyce and Nora did have a sexual relation, says Lacan—she fitted him like a glove turned inside out. But he did not appreciate her as a symptom. What does this mean? Take a glove, turn it inside out and put the other hand inside it: it adjusts marvellously well, fitting exactly. This is how well Nora "fitted" Joyce, for Lacan. However, given the way that Lacan defined the presence or absence of a relationship in topological terms, it is unclear how they could have a relationship without a symptom/*sinthome* that makes non-equivalence and a relationship possible.

I think the confusion is between relationship and sexual relation, as well as between symptom and *sinthome*, sometimes used as similar or identical and sometimes used as duplicate and different. The symptom makes a relationship possible, by making a knot between two circles, but at the same time puts the relationship at odds and makes for the impossibility of a sexual relation. Thus, this means that in the case of Joyce and Nora there was a relationship and also a sexual relation. The symptom did not put the relationship at odds, perhaps because the *sinthome* that Joyce constructed in his work made the symptom not interfere with the sexual relation.

> We find in Joyce's letters (Ellman, 1975) the desire to choose clothing for Nora and organise her diet, so that she will end up with the form he wants and demands. (Harari, 1995, p. 165).

So far it sounds like she was the phallus for him.

> As their relationship progresses, the letters take on a scandalous, obscene note; we can read accounts of demands for some fairly bizarre sexual practices, which are hard to distinguish from perversion [...] he wanted to lie down under her anus in order to see how she defecates and to savour her farts and excrement; all that written with an indescribable jouissance [...] "I wish you would smack me or flog me even. Not in play, dear, in earnest and on my naked flesh [...] I would love to be whipped by you, Nora dear!". Furthermore, he often addresses her as my sweet little whorish Nora or something of that kind; and then of course claims never to have known anyone as pure and holy as she [...]. Thus, he writes to his one and only Nora: "O take me into your soul of souls and then I will become indeed the poet of my race" (Harari, 1995, p. 165–166)

Joyce desired to possess Nora's body and soul, to appropriate her completely. We might associate this with entering the body, turning it "inside-out". Again it is difficult to ascertain how this would differ from the muse or the woman symptom for a man who wants to possess her. Joyce also experienced jealousy thinking that Nora could betray him with another man.

> To the question "What was this woman then for this man?" Lacan replies: "She doesn't serve any purpose. It is only through the greatest of depreciations that he made of Nora the chosen woman." The term "depreciation" deserves an explanation. It would appear to contradict all the evidence we have of the esteem in which Joyce held Nora, and also with the patent fact that he used her his entire life. (Soler, 2014, p. 139)

According to Lacan, "depreciation", when it concerns a woman, does not designate a narcissistic minimising or degrading of the characteristic qualities of a person. The term refers to her function as a woman. Depreciation and degradation are not the same word or concept. When a man (male or female) degrades a woman (male or female) and uses her sexually as an object of waste to be discarded or destroyed, this stands in sharp contrast to the woman that he would marry or have a relationship with.

Nora didn't serve as Joyce's phallic armour: it was provided not by her but by his writing. What is implicit in Lacan's affirmation, his postulate, is that the appreciation of a woman consists in raising her to the rank of symptom: in other words, to make use of her for the purpose of jouissance (pleasure and pain). Again we remind the reader that a relationship could not take place without a symptom of non-equivalence.

Joyce, who was beyond all the prejudices of his time, knew how to value the relationship with Nora, her simplicity, her good qualities, her honesty, her imaginativeness, her flexibility in life, but he did not make use of her as a symptom of jouissance, which would have been to appreciate her as a woman. His *sinthome* is his writing.

This is indeed why Lacan could say that she fits him like a glove. For him, symptoms, whatever their benefits of jouissance, never fit like a glove: they put the subject at odds.

Table of terms.

Φ (Phi) φ (phi) Σ (zigma)	Chosen object. Relationship	Symptom +phi Imaginary Sexual act in the absence of a sexual relation	Devalue/Degrade -phi No sexual relation or a perverse sexual act	Value virtue Symbolic Name Phi as a place of substitution	Sinthome Real Zigma
	They had a sexual relation. Depreciate her: Nora is his whore.	Appreciation Phallic woman Is rather than has the phallus. Make her the semblance of the phallus	Ugly, small breast, bad smell, or an object of waste to be used and discarded; "He is not a real man", etc.	Simplicity, honesty, flexibility, valour, etc.	Joyce's work Man or woman as a devastation in the form of the capital Phi of symbolic Castration
	Obscene; shit on me; hit me	Missing in Joyce			Woman as the Real non ex-sisting subject

Closing comment on the false and true hole

Earlier I stated that the discourse of the master becomes undone and needs to become undone like the knot of three. The master is like the strike of the Real in the knot of three that needs to be replaced by a new invention of the *sinthome* which is the NoF coming from the Real.

The invention of the *sinthome* appears to constitute a new advance, a new conception that goes beyond the logic of the phallic signifier. Lacan now refers to this invention in terms of the order of the knot of four. Here we are dealing with another dimension than that of the Symbolic.

In this session he says that what traverses the false hole is the straight line which now he identifies with the phallus. The phallus is what verifies the false hole, and he says that the Real is the false hole, without mentioning that the *sinthome* makes the false hole into a true hole that is beyond the logic of the signifier. Now we are back to only a false hole and the logic of the phallus.

In my opinion, this is a contradiction that can be thought of in terms of the phallic function of capital Phi rather than the small phi of the imaginary phallus. The capital Phi of the symbolic phallus leads to the signifier of a lack in the Other which within the Symbolic is a false hole that leads to the true hole of the Real, the *sinthome*, and the Name that emerges from the Real. The false hole can lead to a true hole because inside the false hole there are both type of S_1 signifiers, the phallic signifier and the imaginary *objet a*, but S_1 can also represent the *objet a* in the Real that leads the subject to a true hole within the Real and to a jouissance of Being beyond the phallus.

Commentary on sessions 9 and 10 of Lacan's
Seminar XXIII
Wednesday 16 March 1976 and Wednesday 13 April 1976

The bladder and the lantern
The outside meaning and the foreclosed meaning

L acan in this session is looking for an easy way to approach
Joyce, an "*a*-Joyce", and "*a*-Freud", and we could say an
"*a*-Lacan". The *a* in this case represents the privative *a* or
a negative or a negation/symbolic castration in the sense of not
being able to approach and understand the work.

At first we read Lacan and we don't see an easy way into
the seminar. We read the words but do not understand. But at
some point this non-understanding produces what Lacan calls
a Real cool heat lantern that turns our understanding.

What is the easy way?

A straight line, another or a second straight line, and a third
straight line that is bent or becomes a circle, in other words
a Borromean knot.

The Real comes in bits. A bit (*bout*) piece of the Real and
an interval of short duration. An instance/instant in no-time,
a nanosecond or a no-second, or a gap between two moments.

A good way to conceptualise the conundrum of the Real
is to use the example of some of the findings of contemporary physics. This would be consistent with Lacan's interest
in matter and materiality. The use of physics in this book, in

my opinion, doesn't really correspond to how physics is used in neither of the contemporary discourses that Žižek (2005) mentions: cognitive science, postmodernism, or New Age ideology. The Real in Lacan does not correspond to either hermeneutics or constructivism and the view that everything is interpretation, nor the sense of objective reality and theory that prevails in modern science. Gödel already proved the incompleteness operating within mathematics which shows that there will never be a total correspondence between the ratio and concept of Reason and the truth that lies in the nature of things. We will never know everything or have a theory of everything. The theory is not always right about everything whether we are dealing with numbers, concepts, or metaphors. The Real, the symptom, and the quantum level of reality will evade objective causality and work more as a principle of randomness and chance that mathematics approximates in terms of probability and prime number theory.

The Real of the symptom/*sinthome* is also a form of jouissance that Lacan links to the three forms of jouissance (inconvenient and convenient) including the third jouissance of the mystic and feminine sexuality that are forms of experience close to the reality of things in themselves without constituting an essence or a concept. Jouissance is a pure sensitivity without representation. However, as distinct from the jouissance of the mystic or spiritual experience, the Real for Lacan is also a mathematical structure, as a discourse without words in the sense of symbols or letters rather than stories. On the other hand, human symbols, letters, and Names are also closer to the Real than calculations to infinity in the way that a computer or a robot are able to do using artificial intelligence.

Within mathematics there are numbers that are non-numbers (i.e., i or imaginary numbers), or are not standard numbers yet they function within arithmetical systems. At the same time the Real is beyond mathematics in the sense of there being two different forms of the Real: an interior and an exterior Real. The exterior Real is not objective and the interior Real is not subjective in the ordinary sense of the terms. The interior Real is *extimate* (something intimate that at the same time is foreign to the ego), to use the neologism invented by Lacan, and the exterior Real is transubjective as a form of jouissance. We experience the exterior Real but we know nothing of it. The interior Real can be known as a mathematical truth rather than simply knowledge. The interior Real is a knowable mystery but the exterior Real is an unknowable mystery other than as a form of jouissance.

In physics they are looking for the origin of the universe by looking for the very small "ex-sisting" in the very big and the very big "ex-sisting" within the very small. The very small could be considered as bits or strings of the Real. Within string theory it is said that to physically observe a string as the smallest unit we would have to blow up the string to the size of the entire universe. The very small divides itself into the self-same to create something different in time and space or size. This is also true of fractal mathematics where a simple triangle is reproduced into a million smaller self-similar triangles to create the forms of virtual environments that simulate nature with great realism. This method has given great realism to new forms of animation (Pixar movies would be an example).

There are Q'bits outside time and space parameters and yet also entangled within time space parameters, an exterior and interior Real.

Every object stems from a relation, except for *objet a*. *Objet a* in or on the Real is solitary or a singularity, because it is a no-thing that is empty of inherent nature, of concept and signifier (lack of a concept and a signifier).

Every conceptual object is defined by a relation between x and y, and the relation itself can be described by a z or an epithet which is a word or name expressing a characteristic. For example, language is the Z that describes the relation between x and y or S_1–S_2.

The Real is the object as a no-thing, the Imaginary is the object as either x or y as the referent signified, the Symbolic is both signifiers x and y, and the *sinthome* is the epithet or nickname or the z which emerges from the Real and names the relation. An alternative way is to say that the Imaginary is the object or the constituents, the Symbolic indicates the concepts or variables, and the Z is the empty concept, the number that is not a number, a signifier without a signified, or the concept of emptiness or the arbitrary, contingent, and empty nature of the concept. Z is a Name that can substitute for x or y or that can help substitute x or y for each other.

Lacan uses the example of a bladder and a lantern: things are different but are also the same by virtue of their solitary nature. Lacan uses fire to describe the sameness that can make a bladder a lantern.

A bladder is something inflated and hollow which is actually the definition of empty in Sanskrit. The bladder as an organ also eliminates excess water and waste from the blood. One must deflate or empty the bladder, the bowels, and the vowels of *lalangue*, to make them hollow and orient them towards the Real. At the same time a lamp or lantern is a form that carries a fire and a light.

A lantern is something easy yet has weight and value. How can we manage to present Joyce in this way, a way that is simple or elementary yet complex at the same time, like nature? How do we light our own lantern from his lantern?

Lacan had a dream that he was doing this but he was doing it by not being there, by being an empty Lacan. The dreamer is not any particular character: it is the dream itself. This is the easy way to judge characters, to judge characters such as Joyce, or the characters in Joyce's writing.

How to judge characters not idiosyncratically and in our own image but rather by dissolving or getting our own image out of the way not worrying about our worthiness or recognition in the analysis of the Other.

To do otherwise is to try to give literature and writers and people both simplistic and personalistic story-based interpretations or what Lacan calls a psychodrama.

The best one can do to express the confusion of the sexual relationship is to take a bladder for a lantern.

How to "con-fuse" or fuse emptiness or something hollow or meaningless with light or as equivalent to light, and how to describe or define light in terms of hollowness or emptiness? How to describe the phallus as a lack, or as a vessel with a hole and light in it, and lack as phallic in nature because the vessel can be inside like a bladder or outside like a lantern? The answer to this question perhaps will or must always remain ambiguous.

A fire has to be placed inside a bladder to confuse it with a lantern. The lack is what both sexes share or have in common, whether as a signifier of a lack or the lack of a signifier.

The fire comes from the Real and is a mask or a grimace of the Real.

A phenomenon is a fact, situation, an act, object, or state. Now what is the epithet, mark, or characteristic of a phenomenon?

A mark can be the mark of an object that follows from a structural concept, or a mark can be the mark of the unmarked, the mark of no mark, or the mark of emptiness. Here in this moment, gone in the next.

The first one has the mark pointing at so-called objective reality while the second points to the Real.

When the two are confused, then the mark of the object becomes the mark of nothing or a mask and grimace of the Real.

A phenomenon is a flashing of light, a phantom or a *"fan-thomas"*, a holy ghost, appearing and disappearing.

Fire, as a mark of nothing rather than as a mark of the sun or of burning fossils, becomes the same as a cold fire, an absolute zero. Is the universe expanding to a deep freeze or contracting into a great fiery explosion? What is the probability of one or the Other? Because we don't understand we think in terms of the phantom or *daemon* of chance but the Real is a *tyche* (the two types of chance described by Aristotle), a true hole instead of a false hole.

Lacan says heat has no upper limit but that the absence of heat or coldness has an absolute zero, and thus it is absolute zero that establishes an orientation and a true limit.

But if the Real is a fire then the absence of fire/heat is just as much a fire (however invisible) as the infinity of heat. "Nothing" is hot. Light can become a black hole or an absence of light that contains light in the infinitesimally small. Even in the vacuum of space there are virtual particles that burst in and out of existence before they can coalesce into matter. Those virtual particles if sufficiently accelerated can be turned into light (photons). However, the void has less energy than everything else and this small amount of energy state keeps the void and the universe stable and constant. In addition, if you point the Hubble telescope to a dark patch of space and zoom in, eventually dim stars and later galaxies will appear in your sight.

The orientation of the Real has no meaning or its "sense" is precisely the orientation of emptiness or senselessness, the mark of no mark or the unmarked.

The different senses are coordinated by each being more than their main characteristic, the eye sees, the ear hears, but seeing and hearing includes the orientation given by the Real of no sense or senselessness. As Lacan said, it is the Real that links the senses together. But now we need a new Name, epithet, nickname or proper name for this Real. But even if we come up with a name for it, the Real will never be a common point between the senses. The Real is found within each of the senses as a null set and this is what they share in common.

In a previous session Lacan said that the Real is what links the Symbolic and the Imaginary together which otherwise would remain separate and exclude one another. Now he says that it is the copulation of the Symbolic and the Imaginary that produces meaning and that the Real excludes any meaning. So the Real would be like a catalyst that helps generate meaning and at the same time remains outside of it.

The Real is outside meaning because it has no meaning but by having no meaning it generates meaning by linking the Real to the Symbolic in the act of nomination. The symbolic connotations of a Name are suppressed and emptied out. In the example of Buddhism, or of the historical figure of Siddharta or Gautama, once an undefinable awakened state was realised, Siddharta is re-nominated or called Buddha (awake). After his enlightenment, when he was asked who he was, he said: "I am awake". The new name (Buddha) then is inserted back into the symbolic order of a tradition and the common word awake acquires a new significance. Awake signals a realisation rather than simply the state of not being asleep. You can be awake while you sleep or be asleep while conscious.

Lacan uses the term foreclosure of meaning but this is a different meaning than the one used by the foreclosure of the NoF which alters the relationship between signifier and signified. If the symptom is metaphorical, by contrast nomination does not work according to a pattern of substitution: it is not a replacement of anything else, but sets itself up for and by itself as a solitary letter or unary trace of the signifier that has significance rather than signification and the meaning of which is enigmatic. The signified is in the Real rather than the Symbolic. Such letter has clarity and radiance as a state but the meaning is cryptic and not necessarily clear.

Miller (www.lacan.com/frameXX2.htm) has written about the question of the relation between the Symbolic and the Real. He thinks of naming as a supposition.

> It is the supposition of the agreement of the symbolic and the real. It is the supposition that the symbolic agrees with the real, and that the real is in accord with the symbolic.
>
> Naming is the pastoral of the symbolic and the real. Naming is equivalent to the thesis of knowledge in the real, or at least it's the first step, the significant one, in the direction of knowledge in the real. The proper name is an

anchoring point, not between signifier and signified, but
between symbolic and real, from which we find ourselves
with things, that is to say with the world as imaginary
representation.

The so-called accord between the Real and the Symbolic is
biased towards the Symbolic and through the Symbolic the
world appears as an imaginary representation of the Real.
Otherwise we know from Lacan that the Symbolic will resist
the Real by using the Imaginary to suture the gap that the
Real opens in the Symbolic. A table becomes a table as a word
and an image perceived by the mind/brain when in fact we
don't know what a table really is. The S_1–S_2 is both a word and
the image of an object. The Real is reduced to a S_1–S_2 relation
within language and is no-longer enigmatic. In the enigma
there is an element of chaos and chance in language that devi-
ates from normative meaning yet it does not destroy language,
as is the case in psychosis. The enigma regenerates language
by leaving open the hole within language and within images
that leads to a sense of the Real immediacy and self-external
nature of things.

When a defence comes to bear on the source of repression
or primary repression, then the term is foreclosure, but when
the defence comes from the action of the NoF then the term
is primary repression. So repression and foreclosure seem to
preclude one another. Foreclosure disables primary repression
and primary repression prevents and pre-empts foreclosure.
With foreclosure the Symbolic is disrupted and the Real
appears only in the Imaginary.

Either repression and foreclosure are different types of
defence or the different defences are different types of repression
including the repression of repression or the repressive turned
against itself. The first thesis seems to be the case given that it is
helpful to think of repression as functioning within the function
of metaphor and substitution typical of the symbolic order.

The outside of meaning in the case of the Real differs from the foreclosure of meaning in the example of psychosis as described by Lacan in *Seminar III*. The NoF and the imaginary phallus as the signified of the NoF are both foreclosed or cut out from the symbolic net and return unmetabolised from the Real of a hallucination. In the example afforded by psychosis the unmarked disarticulates rather than articulates the relationship between the senses. The re-articulation of the senses indicated by unmarked and subtle perceptual experiences points instead to the need to be rid of the NoF by making use of it, as Lacan says in the seminar under consideration.

If we think from the perspective of the independence and difference between the Symbolic and the Real, while knowing that if one changes something on the side of the Symbolic one can have effects in the Real, then the Knot becomes a necessity. The two, Symbolic and Real, can remain two different registers at the same time that they're inseparable. The Borromean knot lets the two elements remain distinct and at the same time they are inseparable because they are joined in a way where they cannot be separated. This point is brought further home with the knot of four in the analysis of neurosis where the knot of three is untied and re-tied with the fourth ring of the *sinthome*. Each ring of RSI can flourish in its uniqueness without being restricted by being tied to the other two. The Borromean form of the knot of four surmounts the antinomy of juncture and disjuncture as Miller has pointed out (ibid.).

We see here what is the peculiarity of the knot in relation to the chain. The knot and the chain are two forms of articulation, but in the knot the elements remain connected yet independent. In a chain, binary elements are typically connected and bound on two sides leaving little room for each element of the chain to function independently from the other.

But through the knot not only do the two orders remain related but also go into each other. There is the Symbolic within the Real and the Real within the Symbolic. The Symbolic within the Real represents the instance where language covers over the undefinable, inconceivable, and indeterminate nature of the Real either with words or images. Words here don't hit their target and remain empty or idle in the bad sense of the term. The more you speak, the less you say.

The Real within the Symbolic points to two events: a jouissance within language and the matheme as a senseless form of cipher. The matheme, mathematical symbols, and topology make something of the Real transmissible but at the same time what is transmitted is only a bit and not the end of the exterior Real that otherwise remains undefinable within experience.

Lacan says that the Real that is not cognised by the bit and that remains inconceivable or unknowable coincides with Freud's notion of the unconscious in the sense of the unknowable and with "being It" rather than "having it". One cannot be it or one should be it without knowing it. Being it and self-consciousness preclude one another. In addition, what does It represent: the Phallus, *Das ding*: the thing, or the no-thing? Being the phallus, or the archaic object in the Imaginary is only a semblance. But being the unconscious or the no-thing is something different.

The darkness or the shadow aspect of the image (the dark room of photography, for example) that allows the image to be seen represents its lack of self-consciousness or self-recognition, or the fact that the essential (empty) shadow seems to be left out of the perception of the image. Light is dark but we don't see it as dark and dark is light but we don't see it as light. The shadow can be the unconscious side but the unconscious or darkness can represent the repressed id or "It" can also represent the unknowable and undifferentiated.

Knowing how to act or *savoir faire* represents not only deliberation but also acting not only on the basis of the repressed but also on the basis of the Real of a praxis or the unknowable Real manifesting in an act rather than in knowledge. The scansion of speech and the cut of the session are examples of the crossing or the intersection of the infinite line that also brings the infinite line into existence.

The sexual act is both an acting out of a fantasy and a Real act that can bring new life and new death into existence. The copula in linguistics is a link or a tie and the main copula is the verb to be. We are, we exist thanks to the primal scene that remains unconscious and this is how the unconscious proceeds according to Lacan.

Of this Real act only unary traces of the subject and the object remain which are then effaced by an ego discourse and by history and storytelling. Lacan says that behind history lies myth which are traces or bits of knowledge about the Real. These bits are separated again from history in the form of trash or objects of waste that can be recycled once again. In fertilising manure shit once again recovers its status as *objet a* after it had decayed to the form of a reactive character trait of the ego and of discourse.

Cycles, circles, goings around, the beginning is the end, the end the beginning, there is no progress except that marked by death where there is no before and after. The Real like death is impossible and unthinkable.

Lacan says that feminine eroticism culminates in the wish to kill and castrate a man. The copula is represented by the symbolic phallus as something that is missing or does not exist. The phallic function is the function of castration not of copulation or the function of the copula of being is non-being or "disbeing". Castration for a man because the phallic function inhibits first before it facilitates phallic jouissance, and for a woman because copulation represents not having for a woman or the enjoyment of not having or of a cut that can also manifest in the form of a complaint.

The other as unconscious object causes a loss or a jouissance in the subject. The subject is divided and castrated by their own unconscious object. If castration is accepted then the phallus emerges out of the being of the cut: it exists because it does not. Neither the phallus nor the Other (that could respond as a partner) ultimately exists and this exemplifies the relation between the capital Phi of the phallic function (of castration) and the signifier of a lack in the Other.

The barred woman does not exist because she is Real and like God only "ex-sists" or does not exist, either way, as a form of jouissance. Otherwise the symbolic mother of humans for Lacan exists as a layer or as a structure, or more precisely as the hole that articulates the structure of existence.

Session 10 of April 13th, 1976 coincided with Lacan's birthday or the anniversary of his birth. He was seventy-six years old and this was the twenty-second year of his seminar which begun when he was fifty-four.

He brings up the question of energetics. He says it is nothing but the manipulation of numbers as chiffers or figures which are both a number and a figure or a form. In physics it is called a particle. The form of small matter and its corresponding number. According to Einstein (E)nergy=mass plus the speed of light squared (mc^2). Particles can be particles or can also be waves or energy fields.

What is energy in biology? Vitality, the ability to do work. For Freud energy represents a demand for work that the body imposes on the mind. The mind responds with mental activity in the form of thoughts, images, fantasies, as representatives of impulses and drives that seek connections or their destruction.

Lacan says that the Real is a traumatic forcing of a writing that has a symbolic bearing, something that one has to bear, that may be bearable or more or less unbearable, a jouissance, a satisfaction and a dissatisfaction or a frustration. Both the satisfaction and the frustration may be traumatic. He then distinguishes between reminiscence and remembering as mental responses to the demands of the body.

Reminiscence is a kind of imaginary or hallucinatory function of memory as fiction or a form of screen memory that looks like memory but also constitutes a wish marked by the impact of a frustration.

"Re-membering" already implies a structured symbolic world, a copula of letters and signifiers. Remembering implies a study and review of the record although the record may be interpreted via the lens of imaginary wishes and fantasies.

The Real is more like a phonological symbol or function while the signifier conforms a knowledge and a subject that is in conformity with reality. The resource of language allows one to imagine and to say that one has a memory.

In the same way one imagines that one chooses to speak a language although we create each language as we speak and give it a little prod.

We must say that one has a memory and this is an attempt to find the constant or the constant figure or number.

One is always calculating to reach the Phi number without succeeding other than by finding a name that helps us remember. This is finding the number and the letters of an energetics or finding the constancy principle in the drive as a principle of quiescence that allows for memory and reversibility. To keep the number constant in the Name. To transform a death drive into a life drive. To find the lowest possible tension that supports life and keep it constant. The *sinthome* is such a tension that we must keep so that we may remember and live. Science is this Phi number and Name or *sinthome* that helps us remember. Phi is an irrational number where the decimals go to infinity (1.618 ...), so the way to stop the calculation of more numbers is simply to call the number by its Name: Phi, which Lacan makes coincide with the symbolic function of castration.

Language creates a contradictory reality (the antithetical meaning of primal words) no different that when we say that a line is straight and we call it a straight line even though it is bent or circular in the end. The same is true of a ray of light.

The Law in the end is the law of emptiness or the law of form is formlessness, or the mark is the mark of the unmarked. The Real is without law and the Real is not the Symbolic and the Symbolic is not the Real.

Commentary on session 11 of Lacan's *Seminar XXIII*
Wednesday 11 May 1976

Two types of writing and ego function
The knot of four in neurosis and psychosis

The Borromean knot must be written. Why? Because the knot as well as the signifier is a support for thought or for non-thinking or *appensee* (the *a* as a privative a). Writing is a doing which gives support for and precipitates thinking.

The Bo (Borromean) knot must be written in order to get something from it.

Lacan describes two types of writing:

Writing with the signifier and writing degree zero or in a state of erasure. It does not cease from being written and does not cease from not being written.

This is the characteristic of the NoF emerging from the Real as a unary trace. On the one hand a trace is written, on the other hand, the trace is a unary form of negation because it negates and erases what it negates. It is an affirmation that negates the unmarked or the Real by marking it with a trace or mark. The unmarked refers to the outside meaning, but also to the generation of pure desire and the object cause of desire that is both signified and negated at the same time. The NoF as Signifier, the phallus/*objet a*, and the desire of the mother as signified are written but they also wind back to something Real beyond signification. This Real does not cease from not being written and yet the signifier never stops writing it. What I am calling writing degree zero (following Barthes' (1953) title), is the writing of the Borromean knot, that incorporates the unsayable into its structure.

Because of this fundamental ambiguity associated with writing, truth is both constantly being half said and not being said at all within language.

Lacan says that truth is "repressed" in two ways.

1. It cannot be said. But here the lack of truth is a true hole because the lack is not a product of repression that generates a substitute signifier of lack. In this case, lack presents or manifests a jouissance of a "no-thing" that lacks signifier, object, and concept.
2. The signifier is the substitute signifier of a repressed signifier of an object cause of desire that constitutes a truth of desire for the subject. The imaginary phallus and the imaginary *objet a* are two kinds of repressed objects that appear in the gap or false hole of the Freudian unconscious. The latter is a false hole because there is a false gap or hole in consciousness where the repressed or absent objects/signifiers manifest.

Philia/love/jouissance is the interval or the no-thought or the mind (nous) of free-floating awareness that contemplates and transforms signifiers and writing into thinking. Time is what transforms a thing into a concept/word/thought and at the same time the thing withdraws from the concept and remains as a naught or a gap in thought in a different synchronic dimension of time.

The Bo knot is a mode of writing the Real of the thing that supports thinking and where thinking is supported by something Real or by the Real hands and feet of thought.

This writing is represented by the straight line, or the mark, the tracing of a letter that is also a circle with a hole in it. A form of writing or what for Lacan constitutes a new enigmatic ego that ties the Real and the Symbolic together.

Figure 14. Circle and line.   Figure 15. Circle and cross.

This form of writing is also a logic of sacks and cords that helps us understand how Joyce functioned as a writer.

A sack is a circle that has a third dimension, in other words, a sack is a sphere.

A body and the unconscious and the unconscious body are foreign circles or straight lines or true holes that one has. The body and the unconscious function autonomously on their own although the subject also interacts with them. The body as the organism and the image of the body constitute a body-mind relationship. The image of the body is a psychical representation, an ideal-ego as Freud called it. The unconscious organism is the unknown reverse inside that has to be cut in order to be revealed. Without the cut the organism appears to be absent or inside the holes of the body. For Lacan, the unconscious and the organism function as a false hole. The organism is unknown and appears not to be there but is neither repressed nor beyond representation.

The *image* of the body functions as a cork that plugs the hole, a unary trait that builds the person and the personality. The body image carries the unconscious body into the image of the body in the form of affects, likes and dislikes, attachments and detachments from the image. The total experience associated with these factors needs to be cut and broken up in order to reveal the signifying order that mediates the relationship between the organism and the immediacy of the Imaginary.

The non-attachment to the image of the body as it were the peeling of a fruit skin, or the falling of a ripe fruit from the tree, is something that is left over from the possibility of a relationship to the body as foreign and unconscious. Our body does what it does. One has a body, although it is possible to identify not only with the image of the body but also with the body itself: "I am this" or "You are that".

The identification with the image of the body leads to the belief in a soul and a self. Narcissism is built on the support for the image. To de-identify with the image is to realise and awaken to the reality of no soul or self and to deconstruct narcissism. To simultaneously let go of the objectification of the self and realise and be verified by the self-nature of things.

The ego function or the new I in the case of Joyce is marked by the fact that the image of the body is not involved although the subtle body still functions. This is in contrast to the first ego in Freud which in the form of the ideal ego is a bodily ego but as a surface or image. Because we identify with the body image we relate to the other through the assumption of similar images and minds and selves. Nietzsche (1885–1887) said something similar when he wrote: "The assumption of similar cases presupposes 'similar souls'" (p. 276). Soon these assumptions crystallise into concepts leading to the cognitive ego functions of affirmative judgments of attribution or negation: I am this, and you are not or I am not that and you are this, or this is inside me and that is outside.

What Lacan calls the "osbody" (the osseous or bone body— the spirit is a bone), the writing with and on the bones (i.e., the Ishango bones from the Paleolithic era found with traces and prime numbers written on them) is well depicted by the mathemes for the ideal ego and ego ideal: i(a) and I(O). The ideal ego or the image of the body occupies the place of the a or the "osobject". In this seminar the *objet a* appears as a bone which is part of the unconscious body represented by the image in the same way that the specular image of the body stands in the place of the mother's object of desire. The bone as a symbol of the unconscious organism gets duplicated into a symbolic body of signifiers. The bone is in the place of the *objet a* which is written with images and words (i[a] and I[O]) respectively. Images, ideas, and ideals (of self and self-concepts: ego-ideal) are added unto and wrapped around the body. At the end of analysis, the i and the I can be detached from the *a* and the O. This non-attachment signifies having ideas and ideals without idealisation or fixed identifications, to have a father ideal without an ideal father. The Imaginary is separated from the Real (i/a) and from the Symbolic (I/O), freeing the three registers to be re-articulated under the *sinthome*. The Real becomes the Real of the later Lacan: without the Imaginary of "the thing" and the fantasy of the imaginary phallus, the Imaginary becomes the creative Imagination, and the Symbolic contains the Real or where words hit the Real rather than cover it.

Accordingly, the ego in Joyce functions in a different way. How is this written in the Bo knot according to Lacan?

The Bo knot is a "père-version" (a version of the father or *père* in French) or a form of love for the father as the carrier of castration and of the Law. This is one of the paradoxes conveyed by Freud's and Lacan's teaching: how is it that the castrating father, the father of the no, can also be loved or at least simultaneously loved and hated. An example of this would be when a child says to the father: "I hate you daddy." But ultimately there is no castrating father only a capital Phi function which represents the place beyond castration and the lack in the Other, the signifier of a lack and the lack of a signifier, respectively. Castration is only a symbolic function that in fantasy is represented by the image or the reality (small r) of a castrating father. The Phi function is the place of a missing signifier and the lack in the Other, the signifier of a lack and the lack of a signifier within the symbolic order that provide access to the dimension of the Real which Lacan says is a plenitude beyond castration. The Bo knot represents the love for a function which is always met not without some degree of ambivalence.

In the example of psychotic structure, because of an error in the knot, the imaginary can become untied, and the imaginary relationship then has no place, as in the case of Joyce not being bothered by getting a beating. The function and the body are there but without fantasy or signification. The imaginary body drops off, as distinct from the Imaginary prevailing or having dominion over the Real or the Symbolic. In psychosis there is no Oedipal structure proper because the NoF that establishes it was foreclosed. In neurosis, or so-called "normal" subjectivity, the place of the capital Phi function, the function of the Name is in place, it is not foreclosed but lies beyond representation and thus provides a space beyond castration, Oedipus, and neurosis.

In the case of Joyce his writing as a *sinthome* functioned as the NoF from the Real that prevented the psychotic structure from being triggered or precipitated. Obviously the Imaginary functions differently in both cases. In the knot of four in psychosis the Imaginary is still loose although the imaginary is tied to the Real and the Symbolic through the *sinthome*.

What accounts for the difference in the function of the Imaginary in both cases? In both cases there is a different relationship to the image of the body and to the imagination, but since the *sinthome* is not a complete cure, in psychosis, *lalangue*, language, writing, and thought could remain prone to regressive slippages to malevolent forms of *lalangue* and delusion. In the example of neurosis, the effects of nomination could still remain prone to the narcissism of the ego ideal and making a name for oneself and demanding recognition from the Other. The lack in the Other could be resisted and the bar on the Other could alternate between appearing and disappearing, giving off the impression of both a consistent and inconsistent Other.

Finally, since the knot of four in neurosis, in my opinion, requires that all three rings be untied, this could lead to a more radical and paradoxical form of dissolution, before the *sinthome* ties the Borromean knot back together into a new structure. This is the experience that people may have in analysis of unreality, of not-knowing what is real/Real, of not-knowing which symbolic order to follow or appropriate, and what constitutes fantasy, fiction, or virtual reality, and what constitutes trauma and social environmental reality. The psychotic may have more difficulty doing this since a delusion provides more certainty and deception regarding the symptom and leads to a collapsing of the difference between social and psychical reality.

Let's take another look at the two knots. These knots were assembled, disassembled, and put back together during the course of a seminar using pipe cleaners. Lacan said that to understand topology the knots had to be made with ordinary materials. This is an example of a Real practice. The first knot represents the psychotic structure where the imaginary is loose because the imaginary phallus that the child was for the mother was not "castrated" and the symbolic NoF was not installed due to its foreclosure (see Figure 16 below).

The imaginary function of the father or the NoF that produces repression and imaginary castration and desire as a lack has not occurred as a formative moment of subjectivity. The acquisition of language is compromised although language

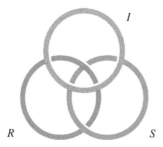

Figure 16. Knot of three psychosis.

and the Symbolic are still there linked to the Real. Moreover, why does the Real in psychosis appear as something imaginary within perception and the Symbolic is found in disarticulated form? The Imaginary is not linked to the Real, so it loses its Real consistency. The Symbolic needs the Imaginary to install the NoF or for its articulation and in psychosis the two registers are not linked.

In the topological image below, with the *sinthome* and the knot of four the psychotic structure is stabilised, but the Imaginary still remains unlinked to the Real or the Symbolic.

Figure 17. Knot of four psychosis.

Lacan asks why Joyce is unreadable? He responds by saying that Joyce evokes no imaginary sympathy or empathy in us. The pleasure/unpleasure ego does not function in his case.

In the particular non-geometrical face of the Bo knot, the ordinary image of the face is emptied out and because it is emptied out it is not obvious that it is a particular human face.

It is a matter of an ego with enigmatic reparative functions. Joyce is the writer *par excellence* of the enigma. The subject cannot be defined according to whether he has a body like an object or a piece of furniture. The subject is defined according to the relationship to the signifier. The ego is defined by the symbolic unconscious in relationship to the Real rather than the Imaginary.

Figure 18. New ego.

Thanks to the mistake, or the dropping of the imaginary body of identity, the unconscious and the Real are knotted together by the new ego or *sinthome*. In the knot above, the vertical line is the unconscious, the circle in the middle is the new ego, the horizontal line is the Real, and the hanging circle is the Imaginary.

Concluding statement on the treatment of psychosis

Each individual in their development goes through steps in the evolution of a symbolic, linguistic, cognitive, and numeral system emerging out of the Real or what was there before representation otherwise known as the unmarked or the outside meaning or sense.

The numeral system begun with the unary trace which both represented and negated the unmarked Real. The NoF is such a type of unary trace that constitutes the root of the cognitive and linguistic system. This is the subtle metaphor that is missing in psychosis, which does not mean that they don't know their name or the name of their father or that they cannot speak a language. Because they lack this subtle metaphor that orients and establishes the system of signifiers and numbers, their language is incoherent or does not make sense because it is driven to represent something that is outside sense.

The NoF is a memorable face/trace of the spirit that carries a voice effect or the legitimate Mark of the unmarked in the voice. It is a soft force under so called normal conditions because it is not easily detectable like the smallest particles of matter in the universe which are nonetheless responsible for most of the radiation of energy that exists. The Real is outside meaning for most people and from this perspective the Real unconscious may be an ordinary experience.

The subtle certainty represented by the NoF in the neurotic will be made uncertain through a process that involves the desire of the mother, the imaginary phallus, and the repression of the two in the production of a battery of signifiers, including vulgarity within language.

What precipitates the psychosis after the original foreclosure of the NoF, is the re-introduction of the NoF as a strong force rather than a soft force, a strong name for reality or fantasy instead of the Name that may turn the experience of the Real into something benevolent. This is what makes for the iatrogenic effects associated with the institutionalised treatments that seem to impersonate the persecuting and constricting figures of the paranoid delusion. Commanding and aggressive super-ego voices both inside and outside the mind, populate the mind and the environment of psychoses. On the other hand, softer enlightened environments in the treatment of psychosis may function as a *sinthome* that helps symbolise experience for the psychotic subject.

In the treatment the clinician has to find ways to construct the paternal metaphor. The symbolisation of the false hole has to be done in such a way that still leaves the true hole in place. If the hole is sutured in a way that closes the hole, then it becomes a persecuting hole. The Real as a true hole has to be signified with a subtle metaphor of the NoF but not as a strong authority principle which is already there in the paranoid construction.

The use of construction also involves giving the psychotic not only a metaphor but also a theory and a narrative of who they are, and where they come from, similarly to a more functional delusion that can be used to live in society. With the psychotic, construction is used to build the missing links between signifiers rather than using free association to reveal the links that are already there.

Community integration, a laudable possible goal for patients, should not be seen as the ultimate goal for all psychotics. As we have seen, certain symbolic roles can in fact lead to similar psychotic deterioration and we must play a vital role in ensuring that an institution's goals do not interfere with what is in the best interests of the patient. A functional marginality, or a community of isolated signifiers and subjects, or a community that tolerates and supports unique signifiers, may constitute the conditions under which a psychotic individual may in fact be socially productive. But the metaphor for such a community will have to remain a soft or subtle force.

Recapitulating conclusions on the theory of psychosis

The psychotic subject does have an unconscious. In the neurotic the unconscious is created through repression; in the psychotic the unconscious is created through foreclosure.

The unconscious in psychosis involves a failure in the program/knot that articulates the relationship between language and perception. In psychoses, the unconscious is found in perception rather than thinking or wishing.

In the psychotic the imaginary phallus returns from the Real in the form of feeling chosen for a persecution that is also a sign of distinction. But in psychoses there is no metaphor only a concrete substitution. The nobility of the NoF is not there to provide protection, instead the subject is exposed to the raw and profane phallic attribute of the Other and to the mother's desire that is conditioned by the object that objectifies the subject. In the clinic we can see this in patients who feel chosen and persecuted by a powerful brutal Other who wants to hurt them or wants to use them as an object for their sexual enjoyment.

What is unconscious is not only everything repressed …

Lacan states that behind the process of verbalisation there is a primordial *Bejahung*, an admission in the sense of the Symbolic, which can itself be missing.

It can happen that a subject refuses access to his symbolic world to something that he or she has nevertheless experienced, which in this case is nothing other than the threat of castration.

What is not clear and directly said by Lacan is that the primordial affirmation at the base of symbolisation refers to the NoF as a primordial signifier representative of the phallic function of castration. It is not that the subject has been threatened with castration, but that castration is the name for the imaginary mass of feelings, sounds, and ideas that the subject may experience in relationship to the presence of the NoF that symbolically castrates the subject as an imaginary phallus of the mother and castrates the mother's imaginary phallus.

At the same time the signified for the first affirmative signifier of negation is the pure desire of the mother with its accompanying enigmatic sounds and feelings, as well as the object of the mother's desire or the small phi (the *objet a*), which in many instances it might very well be the imaginary phallus.

Foreclosure represents a negation of a first negation that forecloses the possibility of generating a Real square of oppositions and a metaphor between the NoF and the desire of the mother both of which emerge from the Real of a true hole. Foreclosure affects the first negation but also the relationship between the NoF and the Real and the desire of the mother that the NoF represents.

Foreclosure affects the Unary Mark of Negation otherwise known as the NoF. The first negation is the root of cognition and language and the negative capability of differentiating this from that. There are two types of primary repression or Being outside meaning. There is the non-differentiation that is an absolute difference between the signifier and the Real, and then there is the relative symbolic difference between this and that and the negation of this difference. The absolute difference between the Symbolic and the Real supports linkage in the Symbolic because there will always be an S_2 trying to represent the link between S_1 and S_0. In this sense absolute difference between the Symbolic and the Real, otherwise known as the prevalence of the non-differentiated Real over the Symbolic, or the mark of the unmarked as a unary negation, supports relative difference and erases it at the same time. Absolute difference does not cease from being written and from not being written.

Thus when the unary negation is foreclosed then the Real cannot be symbolised by a unary trace that orders the series of thoughts and signifiers and supports difference. If you say there is no difference between this or that then this is not absolute difference. Absolute difference has to be found outside meaning or in the Real with respect to the signifier as well as within the signifying differences or the sensorial differences within perception.

What are we not seeing when we are looking? What are we not hearing within listening or not listening, are we responding to the voice or the words? What do we see with our ears and hear with our eyes? What does the nose know? What taste is not in the tongue? How do we touch the untouchable? This no-thing, the unary trace, or the unary negation represented by the NoF, organises and renews the field of perception and the relationship to the Other. But when the NoF or the unary negation is foreclosed, then the Real and the psychotic thing haunts and breaks down the symbolic order and the order of the senses or of sense which is to say the same thing.

The Real forecloses thinking and symbolisation. The Real cannot be wrapped in thoughts or grabbed with the hand of thought. It can only be intended or signified with a non-thought. But there are two types of non-thought corresponding to the two types of primary repression. There is the non-thought of psychotic thinking, a jumbled mass of ideas, which is the same as primary process thinking, and there is the non-thought within a single thought itself unchained from serial thinking and the pleasure principle.

There is a false hole that breaks the links between signifiers, and a true hole that links signifiers to each other by means of S_1–S_0. This latter thought or unary trace is the subject of the Real which is the same as the NoF as a unary trace and a first unary negation. Thinking on the basis of a unary negation or a non-thought or non-thinking leads to meditative thinking at the origin of Being or a primary form of thinking identical in form to true free association in psychoanalysis. Thus primary process thinking as ordinarily conceived perhaps should be renamed primal archaic thinking as seen in psychoses and loose associations, while free association is a primary or ancient form of thinking on the basis of free association and a free floating attention.

In neurosis the knot of three and the symbolic NoF is in place but ultimately needs to be undone. The undoing of the knot of three may produce moments and places of confusion and disorientation, not unlike "ordinary" psychotic states (not the same as psychotic structure).

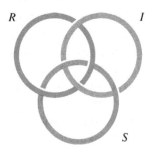

Figure 19. Knot of three.

But with the identification with the *sinthome* in a terminable/interminable end of analysis, a knot of four replaces the knot

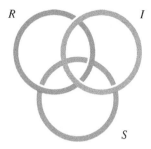

Figure 20. Untied knot.

of three. This is only possible for a neurotic given that for a psychotic the undoing of the link between the Symbolic and the Real (given that the Imaginary is already loose), could aggravate the psychotic condition. For psychotic structure the other type of knot of four is required, as already mentioned earlier. Take a look at the picture below that illustrates a possible and contingent place beyond neurosis.

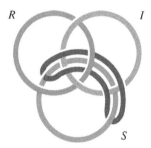

Figure 21. Knot of four neurosis.

REFERENCES

Barthes, R. (1953). *Writing Degree Zero*. New York: Hill and Wang, 1979.

Deleuze, G., Guattari, F. (1983). *Anti-Oedipus: Capitalism and Schizophrenia*. R. Hurley, M. Seem, & H. R. Lane (Trans.). Minneapolis: University of Minnesota Press.

Frege, G. (1903). *Basic Laws of Arithmetic, Vol. II*. P. Ebert & M. Rossberg (Trans). London: Oxford University Press, 2013.

Freud, S. (1894a). The neuro-psychoses of defence. *S. E. 3*, 43–61. London: Hogarth.

Freud, S. (1911c). Psycho-Analytic notes on an autobiographical account of a case of paranoia (dementia paranoides). *S. E. 12*, 3–82. London: Hogarth.

Freud, S. (1912d). On the universal tendency to debasement in the sphere of love. *S. E. 11*, 179–190. London: Hogarth.

Freud, S. (1914c). On Narcissism. *S.E. 14*, London: Hogarth.

Freud, S. (1920g). *Beyond the Pleasure Principle. S. E. 18*, 7–64. New York: Norton & Norton, 1960.

Freud, S. (1923b). *The Ego and the Id. S. E. 19*, 3–66. London: Hogarth.

Freud, S. (1930e). Address delivered at the Goethe House at Frankfurt. *S. E. 21*, 211. London: Hogarth.

Freud, S. (1940a [1938]). *An Outline of Psycho-Analysis. S. E. 23*, 141–207. London: Hogarth.

Harari, R. (1995). *How Joyce made his Name. A Reading of the Final Lacan*. L. Thurston (Trans.). New York: The Other Press, 2002.

Hicks, R. D. (1907). Translation, introduction, and notes. In: *Aristotle De Anima*. London: Cambridge University Press.

Husserl, E. (1983). *Ideas Pertaining to a Pure Phenomenology and to a Phenomenological Philosophy*. F. Kersten (Trans.). The Hague: Nijhoff.

Joyce, J. (1922). *Ulysses*. New York: Dover Publications.

Joyce, J. *Selected Letters of James Joyce*. R. Ellmann (Ed.). London: Faber, 1975.

Lacan, J. (1953). *Book I. Freud's Papers on Technique*. J.-A. Miller (ED.) J. Forrester (Trans.). New York: Norton, 1991.

Lacan, J. (1955–1956). *The Psychoses. The Seminar of Jacques Lacan. Book III*. New York: Norton and Norton, 1993.

Lacan, J. (1956–1957). *La Relacion de Objeto El Seminario de Lacan*. Buenos Aires: Paidos, 1994.

Lacan, J. (1960). *The Subversion of the Subject and the Dialectic of Desire*. In: *Ecrits*. B. Fink (Trans.). Norton, New York and London, 2006.

Lacan, J. (1961–1962). *The Seminar of Jacques Lacan. Book IX. Identification*. Cormac Gallagher (Trans. from unedited French typescripts). London: Karnac.

Lacan, J. (1964). *Seminar XI, The Four Fundamental Concepts of Psychoanalysis*. New York: Norton, 1981.

Lacan, J. (1964–1965). *Crucial Problems for Psychoanalysis. Seminar XII*. Cormac Gallagher (Trans.) unpublished. Lacaninireland.com. Accessed August 24th, 2015.

Lacan, J. (1966–1967). *The Seminar of Jacques Lacan. Book XIV. The Logic of Fantasy*, trans. Cormac Gallagher (Trans. from unedited French manuscripts). Unpublished. Lacaninireland. com. Accessed August 24th, 2015.

Lacan, J. (1968–1969). *From an other to the Other. Seminar XVI*, Cormac Gallagher (Trans.). Unpublished. Lacaninireland.com. Accessed August 24th, 2015.

Lacan, J. (1969–1970). *The Other side of Psychoanalysis. Seminar XVII. (1968–1969)*. Cormac Gallagher (Trans.). Unpublished, www.lacaninireland.com. Accessed August 21st, 2015.

Lacan, J. (1970–1971). *On a Discourse that might not be a Semblance. Seminar XVIII*. Cormac Gallagher (Trans.). Unpublished. www.lacaninireland.com. Accessed August 21st, 2015.

Lacan, J. (1971–1972). ... *ou pire*. *Seminar IXX*. Cormac Gallagher (Trans.). Unpublished. www.lacaninireland.com. Accessed August 21st, 2015.

Lacan, J. (1972–1973). The *Seminar* of Jacques *Lacan*: Book *XX*. *On Feminine Sexuality, the Limits of Love and Knowledge (Encore)*. New York: Norton and Norton.

Lacan, J. (1975). *La Troiseme Jouissance*. *Lettres de l'ecole freudienne, no. 16*: 178–203.

Lacan, J. (1975–1976). *Joyce and the Sinthome*. *Seminar XXIII*. Cormac Gallagher (Trans.). Unpublished. www.lacaninireland.com. Accessed August 21st, 2015.

Lacan, J. (1976–1977a) *Seminar 24 L'Insu que Sait* ... (Love is the Unknown that Knows about the One Mistake). Cormac Gallagher (Trans.). Unpublished. Lacaninireland.com. Accessed August 24th, 2015.

Lacan, J. (1976–1977b). *RSI*. Cormac Gallagher (Trans.). Unpublished. www.lacaninireland.com. Accessed August 21st, 2015.

Miller, J.-.A. Pure Psychoanalysis, Applied Psychoanalysis, and Psychotherapy. *Lacanian Ink 20*. www.lacan.com/frameXX2.htm. Accessed August 21st, 2015.

Moncayo, R., & Romanowicz, M. (2015). *The Real Jouissance of Uncountable Numbers. The Philosophy of Science within Lacanian Psychoanalysis*. London: Karnac.

Nietzsche, F. (1885–1887). *The Will to Power*. London: Random House LLC, 2011.

Romanowicz, M., & Moncayo, R. (2015). Going beyond castration in the graph of desire. *Irish Journal for Lacanian Psychoanalysis, 2015*.

Saussure, F. (1915). *Course in General Linguistics*. New York: Mc-Graw Hill, 1966.

Soler, C. (2014). *Lacan—The Unconscious Reinvented*. London: Karnac.

Spitz, R. A. (1945). Hospitalism—An Inquiry into the Genesis of Psychiatric Conditions in Early Childhood. *Psychoanalytic Study of the Child, 1*: 53–74.

Winnicott, D. W. (1963/2011). *Reading Winnicott*. London: Routledge.

Žižek, S. (2005). *Interrogating the Real*. New York: Continuum.

INDEX

131